EFFECTIVE CORPORATE FUNDRAISING

W. Grant Brownrigg

Foreword by Toni Goodale

American Council for the Arts
570 Seventh Avenue
New York, NY 10018

©Copyright 1982 American Council for the Arts
Additional copies available from:
  American Council for the Arts
  570 Seventh Avenue
  New York, NY 10018

Copy editing by Bruce Peyton
Text design by Linda Dingler
Cover design by Pat Beljanski Gherman, Mayer Visual Communications

Typography by ILNY Communications and Media Corporation
Printing by Edwards Brothers, Inc.

Manager of Publishing: Robert Porter

Library of Congress Cataloging in Publication Data

Brownrigg, W. Grant.
  Effective corporate fundraising.
  1. Fund raising.   I. Title.
HG177.B78   658.1′522   82-3887
ISBN 0-915400-37-5   AACR2
ISBN 0-915400-38-3 (pbk.)

The American Council for the Arts
(ACA) gratefully acknowledges
the generous grant from the
Shell Companies Foundation
for the publication of this book.

\

FOREWORD

Nonprofit organizations in this country should not overlook corporations as a vitally important resource for their fundraising programs. The 1981 Tax Act permits businesses to deduct up to 10% of their taxable income in gifts to charity. Currently, only about one fourth of the nation's corporations give such contributions and most of them only deduct about 1% annually. The potential for growth, therefore, is enormous and some corporate executives have predicted that total giving from the business world will rise from an annual total of $2.6 billion in 1980 to $10 billion by 1990.

There is a certain mystique about corporate giving which leads to an uneasiness on the part of grant-seekers in their approach to the business world. Corporations which do not have foundations are under no obligation to provide information concerning their giving policies. To add to the confusion, companies sometimes give in several different ways: through foundations, staff and board committees, public relations or advertising departments, or directly from the chairman's office.

W. Grant Brownrigg's book *Effective Corporate Fundraising* goes a long way toward dispelling this mystique by providing solid guidance to nonprofits in their approach to corporate funding. Beginning with an evaluation of the philosophy and decision-making process involved, it takes us through all the important steps and defines the tools, resources, and materials needed to build a successful solicitation program.

Unlike foundations and certain governmental agencies, corporations are not established to distribute funds for the common good. They are interested, instead, in promoting a healthy society and in supporting programs and organizations which will show a return on their investment. Mr. Brownrigg gives us a realistic approach which focuses on the necessity of "selling" your case and "marketing" your product, terms which the business community understands and appreciates. Although the book is oriented towards the arts, it includes fundraising principles which have broad applicability to all nonprofit organizations and institutions.

One of the strongest features of this book is its ability to present the grant-making process from the perspective of corporate executives who are responsible for contributions. We become aware of the framework in which they are functioning and of the reasoning and motivation behind their decisions. An additional strength is its description of corporate interviews and how best to conduct them. Armed with this knowledge and with realistic statistics and analyses presented in the text, development officers and trustees have a much better chance of avoiding pitfalls and preparing a successful campaign.

As president of a consulting firm which specializes in corporate solicitation, I have reviewed many articles and books on how to raise funds from the business world. The practical applications of this book, taken together with its unusually perceptive evaluation of corporate funding, should make it a must not only for arts organizations, but for schools, hospitals, and other nonprofits who realize that corporate solicitation should become an integral part of their development programs.

TONI K. GOODALE
President
TKG Associates, Development Counsel
March 3, 1982

PREFACE

This book describes in detail a practical and systematic approach to soliciting contributions from business firms. Its purpose is to provide a down-to-earth, useful tool for fundraising. It is based upon my experiences while serving as the executive director of the Greater Hartford Arts Council and as the director of the American Council for the Arts, as well as on conversations with corporate contributions officers and fundraisers around the country. Although its focus is on the arts, the precepts and methodology of this system have been written in the belief that they are applicable to any type of nonprofit fundraising.

CONTENTS

LIST OF EXHIBITS

1

OVERVIEW

Soliciting contributions is a selling process. As in any marketing effort, an approach must be developed to satisfy the needs and likes of each potential customer. The aim is to convince each customer that the "product" presented to him is worthy of his support and will produce benefits that outweigh the cost. Thus, the basic steps in developing a fundraising strategy are to identify the market and its needs, to determine what you have to offer that market, and to develop an approach that is both effective and efficient in reaching that market.

Because of the abuses by some individuals, selling can have negative connotations, but it should be a positive process, a way of communicating effectively. In the contributions area, this means describing the excellence and importance of your programs — their impact and their quality — in an appealing manner that is easily understood by the potential contributor.

Effective selling or fundraising often involves emphasizing different aspects of a particular program to different audiences; it never involves false statements or distortions, nor does it ever need to affect the content of what is sold. How something is described, what is emphasized and what is not, does not alter what it is. Emphasizing an all-weather system's cooling advantages to someone in the tropics and its heating advantages to someone in the arctic does not change the system's capabilities.

The essential ingredients of a successful fundraising effort are planning, organization, leadership, and hard work. There is no magic, there are no shortcuts to success.

Four fundamental principles underlie the fundraising process and should be kept in mind throughout the development and implementation of an effective corporate strategy:

People give to people. No matter how good the program, fundraising is a personal process. People do not give to a piece of paper or to a building. They give to other individuals — a friend who has asked for help, a business contact, a person who inspires their confidence.

Volunteers solicit; the staff does the work. Because the paid staff member of an arts organization has an obvious vested interest in the program he is selling, his efforts are often discounted by those he approaches. Consequently, effective fundraising uses volunteers who have influence and credibility with the people being solicited. Most volunteers, however, have little time to spend on your efforts and a large amount of natural reluctance to ask for contributions. Thus, the staff must do as much as it can to take care of the fundraising mechanics and details. When the volunteer finally takes time to make his contributions contacts, his time must not be wasted searching for telephone numbers or determining what to say.

Fundraising is the board's responsibility; it is your job. Although securing sufficient financial support is technically the responsibility of the board, it is your personal livelihood which is at stake. Should the drive fail and the organization dissolve, the board of directors may be truly sorry, but you will be out of work.

Nothing is easy, and fundraising is no exception. It requires careful attention to every detail. Names must be spelled properly and assignments made correctly; deadlines must be established and met. You must be sensitive to the interests of each prospective contributor and match those to the appropriate aspects of your program. You must be sensitive to your solicitors and your staff, at the same time making sure that everyone does his job.

This book outlines a practical approach to corporate fundraising by proceeding step-by-step through the four major phases of the fundraising process:

1. Identifying your market and analyzing its expectations and needs (Chapter 2);
2. Determining what you have to offer that market (Chapter 3);
3. Developing an effective and efficient mechanism for successfully reaching that market (Chapters 4–8); and
4. Implementing your strategy (Chapters 9–12).

By carefully carrying out each step described in the following chapters, you can develop an *effective* corporate fundraising campaign.

2

THE BUSINESS MARKET

The first step in developing a corporate fundraising strategy is to analyze the characteristics of your market, the business community. Such an analysis requires an understanding of business attitudes and motives, an awareness of the corporate contributions process, and a knowledge of the various means by which business supports the arts.

GENERAL CHARACTERISTICS OF BUSINESS

Although generalizations about business characteristics have the same shortcomings as any generalizations, they do highlight attitudes and provide frames of reference that will be important in fundraising.

Profit. The focus of business is on making a profit, on selling something for more than it costs so that the company can invest in the future and reward its employees and shareholders. Most corporations believe they can best help the community not by finding ways to give away money, but by making a profit and thereby providing jobs and other benefits that are essential to the community's economic vitality.

Contributions. Corporations recognize only one valid reason for the contributions function: it must help the corporation achieve its overall goals by improving the environment in which the company does business. A healthy business cannot exist in a sick community; consequently, it is in a company's best interest to support worthwhile organizations and activities in the community in which it is based, to which it sells its products, and from which it draws its employees and other resources. Corporations contribute more from enlightened self-interest than for any other reason.

Staff. Of course, corporations are in no way separate from the people who run them — individuals with the same mixture of altruism and self-interest as those who seek funds, people anxious to do a good job, to better themselves and the society of which they are a part. *People* make corporate decisions, carry out corporate actions, and implement corporate policies.

Attitudes. Naturally, the attitudes, opinions, and biases of people who work in corporations are strongly influenced by their working environment, an environment that emphasizes efficiency, linearity, brevity, numbers, and results. Every day, corporate employees are measured by these standards, and rewarded or punished accordingly. The more reinforcement these standards receive, the harder it is for the corporate executive to understand why other organizations do not or cannot operate in the same fashion. ("If it were run well, it would not lose money." "If they were any good, they would have real jobs.")

This does not mean that all executives are insensitive to the needs of those outside the corporate world. In fact, the contrary is generally the case, especially among contributions officers. However, no matter how sympathetic a contributions officer may be to your needs and to the difficulties of a nonprofit existence, he must convince his superiors and his board that your work merits support. Whatever resistance he confronts will be defined by the attitudes described above.

CORPORATE CONTRIBUTIONS TO THE ARTS

The contributions process is difficult to describe because it varies significantly from corporation to corporation, and reflects the strategy and objectives of each company. Moreover, there is little information available on this subject, for corporations only recently have begun to make information on their contributions practices publicly available.

When it is available, a company's annual report is often the best source of information about a company's giving patterns. This will usually list all grants by category (art, health, etc.), specifying donee names and the amounts given. Often included are brief sketches of the funded projects, descriptions which can help you determine how the contributions staff interprets and applies its guidelines.

There are several sources of information on overall giving policies and trends in corporate philanthropy. The Conference Board publishes manuals on contributions management, and conducts an annual survey of contributions by major corporations for all areas of philanthropy. The Business Committee for the Arts conducts a survey every three years on corporate contributions to the arts, reporting both the total amount given and the distribution among various arts disciplines.

A good source of detailed information on over five hundred individual companies is the *Guide to Corporate Giving in the Arts*, published by the American Council for the Arts (ACA). Although the companies in this directory (drawn from ACA's nationwide biennial survey) are not a statistical sampling of the entire business community, the specific information given for each provides a helpful insight into the corporate giving process. The following observations are based on an analysis of the aggregate information reported in the latest edition of the *Guide*. (See Exhibit A for detailed analyses and tables.)

Percentage of Total Contributions Budget. On average, the companies surveyed gave just over 10% of their total contributions to the arts, with the rest going to education, health and welfare, and other causes. Logically, then, 90% of the average contributions staff's time and effort is not focused on the arts. Thus, it is unlikely that a small contributions department will have someone knowledgeable about the arts on staff.

Competition for Funds. According to the survey's comparison of the total number of requests for arts contributions with the total number of arts contributions made, an arts group has a one-in-four chance of being funded. However, this ratio varies drastically from company to company; with some, the chance is less than one in ten.

Types of Activities Supported. The support recently received by most categories of arts organizations or activities seems to be fairly broad-based, according to the responses to the question "What kinds of arts organizations/activities have you recently supported?" As might be expected, almost every company gives to museums and performing arts, and more than two-thirds subsidize public television and radio. Over two-thirds of the companies also fund community arts projects. You are less likely to be funded if you are a literature group, since only 17% of the companies gave in that area.

Kinds of Support. In response to the question "What kinds of support will your company normally consider?" over 88% of the respondents checked general operating support. Capital projects are supported by 73.1% and nearly 71% said they give special projects grants. In addition, 29.3% match employee gifts, and nearly 19% make corporate art purchases. Only 5.5% said they give commissions to artists.

Geographic Location. 73% of the average company's total grants budget was allocated to organizations and activities based in the same geographic area as the company's corporate headquarters. 10% was allocated on a national basis; the balance went to subsidiary and branch communities. Clearly, a company's geographic focus for contributions is primarily the area within which its headquarters are located.

Decision Making at Subsidiary and Branch Locations. Decisions for contributions away from the headquarters location were made by the field office or branch alone in only 19% of the companies surveyed. Decisions were made jointly by the home office and branch in 42% of the cases, but in 39% of the companies these decisions were made by the home office alone. Thus, effective fundraising from branches and subsidiaries requires a good understanding of overall corporate philosophy and the view from headquarters.

Timing of Applications. For companies which specified a particular deadline or "best time to apply," that date or time period falls mostly within the last two quarters of the year. Companies which did not specify deadlines usually receive requests throughout the year and conduct an ongoing process of review and evaluation.

Whether or not there is a deadline and when it occurs is based on the internal policies and procedures of a company. Some may want to spread the workload throughout the year; others may want all the major requests in hand when they are developing their contributions budget for the next year. Often, deadlines are scheduled around the meetings of a company's board of directors.

Application Requirements. Exact application procedures vary widely from company to company, but certain materials are standard:

- *A written narrative* describing the project or organization to be funded;
- *An annual budget*, showing expenses and revenues by category and allowing for comparison with the previous year's budget;
- *The letter from the Internal Revenue Service* stating that the applicant is exempt from taxes under section 501(c)(3) of the Internal Revenue Code;
- *A list of board members*, with their occupations or affiliations;
- *A list of corporate contributors*. (Usually, amounts do not have to be given, although they may be requested later);
- *An audited statement* (In some instances, an unaudited statement prepared by a professional accountant may be acceptable).

Evaluation Criteria. Companies were given a list of criteria and asked to indicate the importance of each in the evaluation of requests for contributions to the arts. Of the fourteen criteria stipulated in the survey, the two receiving the highest rating from the most contributions officers were "impact on the local community" and "geographic location." Companies are concerned primarily with the areas in which they have facilities; in fact, in most instances requests which do not meet these two criteria will not even be considered.

Only after an arts applicant has met these "threshold" criteria does the company's evaluation focus on the quality of the organization or project. Here, as might be expected, the most important criterion is "management capability." Business places strong emphasis on good management. This is the area in which business, for obvious reasons, feels most capable of making judgments.

The fact that "artistic merit" comes only fourth in order of importance points up the dilemma which every request for arts support poses to business: how can the contributions officer, with only a small staff, be proficient in judging artistic quality in a wide variety of fields, particularly since the logic of the average contributions ratio indicates that the staff should spend only ten percent of its time on the arts? While some contributions departments do have people on staff who are knowledgeable in the arts — at least in certain disciplines — many do not. This is especially true of small companies. Overall, funding the arts is an extraordinarily difficult task for business, particularly that part of the process which takes place in the unfamiliar territory of "artistic merit." It can often be rewarding, but the risks are high. To fund the wrong thing — something that is later ridiculed or condemned — is to incur the considerable wrath of both superiors and stockholders.

The next four criteria — "quality of application," "board of directors," "audience size," and "support by other firms" — are important because they provide indirect proof of the worth of the applicant's activities. Like "management capability," these are areas where business can judge according to familiar standards. Together, these criteria ease the burden of evaluating artistic worth directly.

Although not as important as endorsements by community leaders, corporate peers, and audiences, "support by foundations and government" was given a high rating by over fifteen percent of the firms responding. When reviewing an applicant that meets the geographical test, that rates high in its management and *seems* to be worthy artistically, that involves the company's employees and bears enthusiastic endorsements by those most intimately involved, the corporation often turns to government and to foundations for their views.

It may come as a surprise to some that "publicity value" is far down the list in order of importance, but for those who have had extensive contact with the contributions area it will not. High visibility is essential for advertising but not for contributions, where the best long-term publicity will be in funding worthwhile ventures that have a strong, positive impact on the community.

Finally, whether or not a group has "matching grants" is relatively unimportant and is only a factor after everything else has been taken into consideration. Challenge grants and matching programs seem to have a limited impact on a corporation's giving program.

The Approval Process. The entire contributions approval process varies greatly from company to company, depending on its size and philosophy. In small companies, the president may be the only executive involved; in large ones, there are layers of decision making. Usually, the head of the contributions staff has the authority to make certain grants on his own — normally those in the $500–$5,000 range. Many companies also have a contributions committee consisting of three to six senior executives, who must review the contributions budget and approve all grants above a certain level. Larger grants may require the approval of a top executive or the board of directors. In other words, the larger the grant request, the more complex and layered the approval process. A negative decision at any level is usually final; you cannot take the next upward step on the contributions spiral until you have made the one before it.

Ultimately, all contributions budgets must be approved by the company's board of directors; the board's involvement can range from considering only the total contributions figure to reviewing the budget item-by-item.

Processing Time. Between the time an application is submitted and a final answer is given, companies require an average of almost two months for staff review, follow-up questions, and reviews by the appropriate contributions and board committees. This can vary, of course, depending on the deadlines and overall contributions review cycle. In fact, as a result of the high volume of applications some companies receive, and the relative infrequency of contributions committee and board meetings, the approval process can take up to five months. Your corporate drive must allow for a long decision process and must be timed to coincide with when the decisions are made.

IMPLICATIONS AND SUGGESTIONS

Although your chances of getting funding will vary greatly from one company to the next, certain valid and useful inferences regarding overall probabilities can be drawn from the analysis in the previous section. A consideration of these probabilities in the context of the general business characteristics discussed at the beginning of this chapter suggests ways of proceeding which will improve your chances of success.

Probabilities. The available statistics indicate that on the average, it is easier to get funding from a corporation if your organization is located in the same area as the company's headquarters. Even when this is not the case, the headquarters contributions staff will most likely make the final decision, or at least be very much involved in the evaluation process. Consequently, a clear understanding of the corporation's basic funding philosophy is essential. It is not impossible to get funded if you are not in the headquarters area, but it *is* more difficult. And your success in meeting other criteria will have to outweigh a company's strong reluctance to contribute to activities which may not directly benefit the headquarters community.

The probability that the contributions officer may not be an arts person suggests that large, well-accepted arts organizations have the best chance of receiving significant corporate support. This may be especially true in a time of economic difficulties. As far as the likelihood of support for a particular discipline, the past giving patterns of individual companies should be examined closely and with caution. On the one hand, if a company has contributed to a large number of musical organizations, this may indicate a tendency to continue that trend; on the other hand, it may mean that the company has overextended itself in that area. Individual guidelines and annual reports must be studied carefully and contributions officers asked about this before a correct interpretation can be made.

Mechanics. The approval mechanism of a particular company may suggest an appropriate amount for your request or the manner in which it should be presented. Occasionally, the mechanics of the corporate contributions process can be short-circuited if someone on your board has direct contact with an executive in a position to encourage his subordinates on the contributions staff to make the gift. However, even if such a contact is available, it is very important to make sure all the rules and procedures are followed, that everything is done to encourage the contributions staff to be supportive of your request. No one likes to be forced to do something. And a corporate gift is too important to be left to the whim of a single executive, who might lose interest or be transferred.

Corporations, as we have seen, are often unsure of themselves in the arts funding area. They do not want to fund things that are controversial, unsafe. Your board list may help to assuage their concerns and to convince them of your program's merits. The same is true of a list of contributors which, if it includes a number of other companies, particularly those which are well-known and thought to be knowledgeable about the arts, may help to persuade a contributions officer that your organization is worthy of support.

OTHER KINDS OF CORPORATE SUPPORT

Companies support the arts in a variety of ways, both financial and nonfinancial, other than direct contributions. Although not the subject of this book, these alternatives can be very important and therefore should be understood as possible sources of support.

Funding Through the Advertising/Public Relations Budget. If you have a high-visibility project, you might consider developing a proposal for funding through a company's advertising or public relations budget, where publicity value and enhancement of the company's image are important considerations. In many cases, you can receive both advertising support for one project and contributions support for something else, since each type of funding is given for a different reason and usually comes from a different department and budget.

Benefits. Special fundraising events, or benefits, are often used either to attract corporate dollars in addition to those contributed during a regular fund drive or where such a contribution cannot be obtained. Usually, a highly-visible corporate executive is chosen to chair the benefit and to help the nonprofit organization sell tickets at prices often ranging as high as $500.

Employee Matching Gifts. Another mechanism for gaining corporate support is through employee matching gift programs, whereby a company will match its employees' gifts to an organization with a gift of the same amount — or even a multiple of it. If you can involve a large number of employees in your activities, you can generate corporate support that may be available in no other way.

Nonfinancial Assistance. A variety of nonfinancial support is frequently available from corporations. The use of corporate executives during office hours, the printing of brochures on corporate presses, and gifts of used office furniture are typical examples. While these services usually do not involve out-of-pocket expenses, they are not always without cost to both the company and the arts group. For the company, the cost may be measured in terms of the time and effort required to carry out these services. For the arts group, it may be difficult to attract in-kind assistance when it is needed; companies have schedules and priorities for their own work which will always come first. Furthermore, the services provided may not always meet the standards required. Design assistance may be relegated to an entry-level graphics person who knows nothing about the arts. Subscription brochures may be written by the top-flight publicity department of a corporation that knows nothing about direct-mail selling. In short, even "free" services can be costly, and although the area of nonfinancial assistance is an important one to explore, it is not without its difficulties and pitfalls.

3

BUILDING A CASE
FOR BUSINESS SUPPORT

The fundamental question the arts fundraiser must answer is why business should divert its scarce resources from its profit objective and give away money otherwise destined for reinvestment or distribution to shareholders. To tell a contributions officer it is his or the company's responsibility to do so is unproductive. People do not like to be told what their responsibility is; besides, the primary responsibility of the company is to make money and reinvest its earnings. Your appeal must demonstrate that it is important to the company to contribute to the arts (and specifically to your program) in terms of the company's own interests and long-term goals. You must appeal to the company's enlightened self-interest, as well as to the altruism of individual executives. You must show how the arts are important both to business and to the socio-economic environment in which a corporation is located.

IMPACT OF THE ARTS ON BUSINESS

There are four major reasons why business in general is interested in supporting the arts:

The arts improve the quality of life in a community. They make the community a better place in which to live and work; they make it attractive for well-educated, highly motivated people. In fact, a study by the Rand Corporation concluded that in our service-based economy, jobs follow people; people do not necessarily go where the jobs are, but industries gravitate toward locations with a good pool of skilled labor. Therefore, one of the most important investments a community interested in economic development can make is in improving its amenities, its quality of life, its natural and aesthetic environment.[1] Corporations have a vested interest in building a healthy, attractive setting in which to conduct business. They should be willing partners in making this investment.

The arts improve the image of the community and the companies who do business there. The quality of life is connected closely to a community's image — that indefinable aura that makes both individuals and institutions proud of their community and content to stay there. By strengthening the arts and building up a city's image, a company helps to increase the tendency of its employees to remain. A good image for the community also helps to improve the company's own image, since from a company's location, both customers and peers will often infer something about the company itself.

The arts have a substantial economic impact on a local community. Arts organizations are labor-intensive; they employ hundreds of individuals. The arts also make local purchases of goods and services. If you combine the budgets of all the major institutions in an area and the number of people they employ, the figures can be impressive. The arts also stimulate a community's economy through the audiences they attract. Audiences spend money in restaurants and for ancillary services such as parking. The arts make a community attractive to tourists, to travel agents and convention brokers, and often can help to generate millions of dollars a year in visitor revenue.

By corporate standards, the arts industry itself may not be big business. It can, however, employ hundreds of people in a community and is an industry that enhances the environment rather than pollutes it. A business with those same characteristics would have strong appeal for any chamber of commerce or economic development agency. On that basis, then, it is valid to argue for the support of the arts in a community.

VAUGHAN, Roger J., *The Urban Impact of Federal Policies: Vol. 2, Economic Development*, Rand/Kettering Foundation, R-2028-KF, RC, June 1977.

Creativity is essential to good business; the focus of the arts is on stimulating creativity. Graphics and design are only the most obvious examples. The process of management is founded on creativity. Peter G. Scotese, Chairman of the Executive Committee of Springs Mills, Inc., has written eloquently on this subject:

> 'To see more is to become more,' said Teilhard de Chardin.... The creative world helps us see the environment around us. Art and artists speak to us of people, ideas, trends, struggles, values and needs. As we become more aware of art and creativity, we become more alive as human beings, more alert, more tuned in on the job and in our personal lives....
>
> Innovative companies, large and small, are involved in the arts.... I believe their involvement is... both a reflection of their creative approach to doing business and a source of their creativity....
>
> Marketing, research and development, long-range planning, manufacturing expertise and all the rest are vital to the success of a business. But so are creative people and imaginative ideas. And creativity is best fostered in a creative environment....
>
> Involvement in art is simply good business. A company that is doing interesting things in the arts provides its management and its employees with a stimulating atmosphere. Beyond that, such a company makes a statement to the outside world that it cares about the quality of life and is willing to assume some responsibility for providing culturally enriching experiences for the consuming public. This is not a waste of the stockholders' money. It is a prudent long-term investment in the creativity, imagination and growth of future markets and in the communities in which companies have plants and offices.... Corporate America has provided the financial support to make art available to mass audiences. Long term, the investment will have a lot to do with the national taste level, the tone of America, the values that influence our lives and our decisions in the marketplace. This will be good for the corporate world. Business cannot grow in a wasteland of dull, unimaginative consumers."[2]

[2]SCOTESE, Peter G., "An Investment in Future Values," *Chief Executive Magazine*, August 1979.

IMPACT OF THE ARTS ON SOCIETY

In addition to the direct effects the arts have on business, the arts have a substantial impact on the general society:

The arts enrich the lives of the individuals who observe and participate in them. What Peter Scotese says of business and business executives holds true for everyone. The arts uplift, they touch the spirit, they nourish the soul. The arts change us — for the better.

Although there is little hard research in these areas, artists, arts educators, and arts administrators all over the country have seen the effects of art on individuals — on children and the elderly, on the disturbed and the imprisoned, on the middle class, the upper class and the under class. This impact is, in a sense, much of what art is all about, but because it is so personal, so "spiritual," it is difficult to talk about without making everyone uncomfortable. It's like talking about religious faith — something not done in polite society.

The arts add something to the ability of individuals to handle their own lives and to interact with others. In addition to enriching our lives by allowing us to experience and participate in the creation of art, the arts seem to have an important effect on other aspects of our personal and social existences. This is another aspect of the arts which is difficult to verify. In fact, the positive effects of the arts in this regard are most conspicuous when they are absent, when the arts are denied an individual or a community over a long period of time. One problem with the arts is that their impact is so subtle, so long term that, like maintenance, long-range planning, and research, they can be postponed without apparent effect — at least for a time. But the current concerns about the apparent decline in American productivity and creativity and the increase in alienation seem to indicate that we are beginning to see the effects of this postponement.

The presence of strong arts institutions in an area usually results in the presence of good arts teachers. Musicians, who often supplement their incomes by teaching part-time, are attracted to areas that have good music groups—either because of the possibility of employment with a local orchestra or chamber ensemble, or if this is not possible, as a means of staying involved in their profession by interacting with other musicians and by attending concerts. The same is true of other performers and visual artists as well. Good arts teachers, from all disciplines, are an important asset to a community's educational resources.

STATISTICAL EVIDENCE OF
THE IMPORTANCE OF THE ARTS

In some respects, the best proof of all these claims—both those that argue the direct benefits of the arts for business and those which point to the impact of the arts on society as a whole—is found in the statistics that have been gathered in recent years. That the arts are *perceived* as important to business *by* business is indicated by the twenty-fold increase in corporate giving that the Business Committee for the Arts has charted over the years since 1967. The importance of the arts to people in all segments of society is indicated by the results of a 1980 nationwide survey, conducted by the National Research Center for the Arts, an affiliate of Louis Harris and Associates, for the American Council for the Arts, under sponsorship from Philip Morris Incorporated and the National Endowment for the Arts. The study is the third in a series and its message is clear: In overwhelming majorities the general public—young and old, rich and poor, Midwestern and Eastern, urban and rural—consider the arts not only important, but essential.

Attendance figures are the best measure of public regard for the arts, and in that respect the survey confirmed what arts presenters have been experiencing firsthand. For live performances of classical music, theatre, dance and popular music, for example, the proportion of the population that attended two or more times during the preceding twelve months had increased an average of 50% since the 1975 study.

In the area of education, an overwhelming majority of those interviewed insisted that children should receive adequate exposure to the arts, not in some part-time, after-school fashion, but as an integral part of the curriculum. Substantial majorities — as high as 80% in some cases — said that courses for credit should be offered in the arts, demonstrating the conviction that the arts are basic to education in the minds of most people.

Taken as a whole, the results of this latest survey reinforce one of the most important findings in the 1975 study, in which an amazing 84% of those interviewed agreed that "arts and cultural activities are as important for a community to have as libraries, schools, parks and recreational activities."

Still, even if a company can be convinced that the arts are important, it must be made to understand why money should be contributed to their support. If the arts are so popular, why can't they pay their own way? In business, of course, increasing costs — as determined by the general economy — can be offset by increases in productivity. You must make it clear to the reluctant contributor why such improvements are not possible for the arts, and you must do so in the language of business. Pointing out the "labor-intensive" nature of artistic performances is a good example of this approach: A play or symphony written 200 years ago still has to be handcrafted, still requires the same number of performers. Explaining price limitations in terms of market tolerance is another example: Raising admission charges to a level commensurate with actual costs would not only limit public access to the arts but would also be self-defeating in that the resultant prices would be far above what people would be willing or able to pay.

BUILDING YOUR CASE FOR SUPPORT

The preceding section highlights the major reasons the arts are important, provides strong evidence that they are *perceived* as important by the public, and in the light of their popular "success," suggests how best to confront a company's understandable reluctance to contribute support. For a communitywide drive on behalf of a number of arts groups, these statements about the arts as a whole, strengthened with local statistics, may make a sufficient case for corporate support. For an individual organization, however, this provides only a general framework upon which you must build your specific case, and which must relate your activities to the following concerns.

Quality of art, quality of life, and community image. The most powerful argument for supporting an individual organization is the quality of its artistic product. But because art is so subjective and because the typical contributions officer may not be knowledgeable enough to judge the quality of your work directly, you will need to provide indirect evidence of your artistic success, the positive effects your organization has on the quality of life, and your community image. Good reviews in local newspapers provide evidence of your impact on the community; favorable attention in regional or national media demonstrates your importance. Your audience — especially if it includes enthusiastic corporate employees — can be impressive testimony to the direct impact you have on the quality of life. Clearly, all three factors — quality of art, quality of life, and community image — are very much interrelated.

Economic Impact. Depending on the size of your organization and its type, your contribution to the local economy may be significant. Do you have a large number of employees? Are you a major attraction for people outside your community? Do you have figures on the economic impact of the tourists and conventions you attract? On the other hand, you must be prepared to defend your touring program, for example, if a contributions officer suggests that such an endeavor takes money *out* of the community. Can you show that your program is generating incremental revenue, that it provides extra income for your performers? Is it worthwhile simply because of the visibility it provides for your organization, and for the community in which you and the company being solicited are based?

Creativity. In the mind of the contributions officer, your contribution to this area might be reinforced if you provide on-site workshops in creativity for executives, or classes in art, theatre or dance for the children of corporate employees or for senior citizens, the handicapped, or the poor.

Education. Your in-school programs, together with classes held in your own facilities, can demonstrate your commitment to the education of the community's children, as do "after-hours" demonstrations of special skills and talents by guest artists.

Once you have assessed your organization's activities, you must develop a presentation which emphasizes and focuses on the quality, impact and appeal of your work to the audience and community you serve. It should be straightforward, written in clear, concise language and, where possible, supported by statistics.

Because of the inherent bias about the inefficiency of nonprofits, you need to appear more business-like than business. Nothing should be taken for granted; the basic philosophy, structure and parameters of your work should be explained clearly—in terms someone not familiar with the arts can understand. The next chapter describes how to incorporate the specific content of your case into the essential fundraising documents.

4

DEVELOPING THE
ESSENTIAL DOCUMENTS

Your case for corporate support should be developed and presented through four essential documents, each reflecting your understanding of the business market and your rationale for corporate support, which will become increasingly precise as you prepare the documents. Each of the documents — the overview, the outline, the plan of action, and the budget — presents your case in varying levels of detail and from varying perspectives.

THE ESSENTIAL DOCUMENTS

The Overview, in a sense, is an amplified version of the organization's mission statement. It is a brief summary of what the organiation is all about, why it exists, and why it is important. Although rarely used by itself, the overview is perhaps the most important of the four items, for it will become the introductory section for all the literature on your activities. It sums up all that you do and gives the first impression of your organization.

The Outline builds on the overview by summarizing the organization's major functions and activities. While seldom used as an independent, self-standing document, it serves as the structural framework upon which presentations to corporations are based. It is like a photograph of the organization's basic activities.

The Plan of Action includes a list of long-range goals and describes in as specific detail as possible what will be done in the current year to achieve them. It shows how the functions "photographed" in the outline will be carried out over time.

The Budget describes what resources (primarily money) will be necessary to carry out the plan of action. It lists your sources of income and support and outlines how your resources will be allocated.

ANALYZING YOUR ORGANIZATION

If, through systematic planning, your organization has developed operating and long range-plans, you will be able to use them to create all of the essential documents. However, if there is no time for such a comprehensive effort prior to your corporate campaign, the following is an abbreviated, basic approach. Although the procedure as outlined here is applied to the analysis of an entire organization, a similar procedure could be carried out for any single component of your organization if you are raising funds only to support a particular program.

In most instances, the staff initiates and carries out the development of these documents. Full board involvement usually is not appropriate or possible at the earliest stages, although during the process it is very useful to have discussions with selected board members on their views of the organization and of your analysis. Once a reasonably polished draft of the final documents is developed, it should be submitted to various board members for comment. The final draft should, of course, be discussed, critiqued, and approved by the full board.

Inventory. The first phase of the analytical process is taking inventory of what you are currently doing, what you have done, and your immediate plans for the future. As an initial step you can use the survey checklist shown in Table 1 to list your current activities. This can be done by program title only (e.g., Saturday Afternoon Pop Series) or by generic category (e.g., regular performances, student matinees), whichever is more meaningful and specific. The list must be complete; it must cover 100% of your activities, both programmatic and administrative.

The second step is to enter statistics wherever possible under each activity. The figures should be both individual and aggregate (i.e., attendance per performance and attendance per series). They should be drawn from official records wherever possible; where not, they should be carefully estimated, and you should, as soon as possible, develop a system for collecting such information in the future.

The kinds of statistics needed for performances and classes include attendance figures and the number of individual events or sessions, with breakdowns by type wherever possible. For services, you should list the number of groups helped, the number of requests answered, the volume of memos and newsletters sent out. The data on earned income should include its sources, percent of total budget, and trends. The statistics on fundraising should include the number of contributors, total dollars raised, and expenses. Where official records are not available, or incomplete, make educated guesses; approximations are better than nothing.

Program Analysis. The second phase of the analytical process is to make an in-depth analysis of each major program area. Table 2 is a form that has been developed to assist in this effort.

A brief description of the program is followed by an outline of its history. The historical outline includes: a short narrative; a list of awards and honors; excerpts from favorable reviews and letters; statistics on total events and attendance, which can be transferred from the preceding inventory; and adjectives appropriate and effective in describing your program to business. The analysis concludes with a brief statement on why the program is unique and important. Is it the oldest, the biggest, the smallest, the best in quality, the only one of its kind? Does it meet a specific, urgent need or provide a service available nowhere else?

As you develop each program analysis, it is important to remember that the essential documents you are developing are intended for business. Thus, the statistics and the language must be those which a corporate contributor will understand and appreciate. Collectively, these in-depth program analyses form the raw material for describing the organization as a whole.

TABLE 1

SAMPLE SURVEY CHECKLIST

A. Programs & Services

1. *Productions:* performances, exhibits, readings, lectures, tours

2. *Education:* classes, workshops, in-school classes

3. *Technical Assistance:* consultancies, advice

4. *Information Delivery:* newsletter, calendar, mail/phone requests, research

5. *Outreach:* "social service" functions. Arts in schools, hospitals, prisons, etc.

6. *Community Relations:* Advocacy and promotion of arts, talks at clubs, radio programs, etc.

7. *Shared Services:* In-kind assistance, use of facilities at cost or below, shared equipment.

8. *Other*

B. Support Systems

1. *Earned Income*

2. *Fundraising*

3. *Membership*

4. *Marketing/Publicity*

5. *General & Administrative*

6. *Other*

TABLE 2

SAMPLE SURVEY ANALYSIS FORM

Program _____ (title)

1. Description (brief)

2. History

    a. Narrative

    b. Awards/honors

    c. Reviews/letters

    d. Total events

    e. Total audience

    f. Descriptive adjectives

3. Why is it unique/important?

THE OVERVIEW

The organizational overview is the summation of what the organization is doing, why it is unique, and why it should be supported. Once developed, it becomes the standard, introductory description of the organization and is used in all of its literature — the outline, the annual report, brochures, and plans of action. It becomes, in a sense, the organization's verbal logo.

The overview is derived directly from the program analyses previously discussed, from the organization's by-laws and official mission statements and from your own sense of what the organization is. Taking all these together, the appropriate sentences and paragraphs should tell in clear, brief and businesslike terms:

1. What the organization is.
2. What its mission is (what it wants to be known for).
3. Why it is unique and important.

In describing your organization, it is helpful to group activities into sets of two or three. For example, two major areas, each with three activities, is an easier way to describe and remember six functions than a linear listing. Analogies are also good; underlining helps to emphasize the key concepts.

The following are three samples of overviews that have been developed in this fashion:

Modern Dance Company. "The David Wilde Dance Foundation is a dance company and school whose purpose is the development of a new level of artistic excellence in modern dance. Through a unique blend of sophisticated choreography and a strong emphasis on the individual dancer, David Wilde's works celebrate human dignity. The special skills and techniques found in his choreography comprise a highly developed technical vocabulary that joins modern dance with ordinary life and themes from the nation's heritage."

The above attempt to describe verbally a nonverbal art form was a difficult effort. In the end, despite the somewhat intense language, it was accepted by Mr. Wilde as an adequate description of what he was trying to achieve. The contributions officers who received this overview felt they understood what he was trying to do.

Fundraising Arts Council. "The Greater Hartford Arts Council is a service organization. It serves the arts, it serves business, and in so doing it serves the community.

"The objective of the Arts Council is to support and extend cultural activities in the Greater Hartford Region. The Council's primary means of achieving this objective is to raise money from business in an annual fund drive. In addition, the Council provides technical assistance and other nonfinancial aid to arts organizations.

"The Council also serves the business community. Its support of the arts ensures a high quality of life which helps attract good people and firms to the area. Furthermore, the Council's federated appeal frees companies from numerous individual solicitations, and its comprehensive budget review process assures business that all contributions will be well used and fairly distributed.

"In short, the Arts Council helps unite business and the arts in a circle of mutual benefit."

National Arts Service Organization. "The American Council for the Arts (ACA) is a national arts service organization, founded in 1960, whose mission is to promote and strengthen cultural activities in the United States. ACA's major areas of effort—management improvement and general advocacy—serve to accomplish this mission by helping to improve internal and external support systems for the arts.

"In the area of management improvement, ACA seeks to strengthen the internal management of the arts by improving the administrative skills of arts managers and artists, by providing them with essential management information, and by developing management services for their ongoing support.

"ACA's advocacy efforts are designed to increase the external support of the arts by demonstrating their importance and by helping both the public and private sectors develop reasonable policies towards the arts. In addition, ACA works to build and strengthen alliances within the arts as well as between the arts and other segments of society.

"ACA carries out its mission by providing a number of products and services for arts leaders — arts professionals, arts trustees, and arts supporters. ACA is unique not only because of its specific activities, but also because it is the only organization working on behalf of ALL the arts, all across the country."

These are only examples, and there may be stylistic idiosyncrasies that do not fit your organization. But in each case, the basic techniques — using clear, simple language, breaking up long statements into paragraphs, underlining for emphasis and so forth — help make the message clear and appealing to contributions officers. These techniques can be adapted to your needs.

THE OUTLINE

The outline begins with the overview, then adds to it by outlining each major program and the operations of the organization as a whole. Since the outline is not a full, detailed description of the organization and all of its programs, it is usually not used by itself. It is instead the structural framework upon which the annual report and the presentation to corporations may be constructed. Exhibit B contains the outline for the David Wilde Dance Foundation and the American Council for the Arts.

PLAN OF ACTION

The overview and the outline describe what your organization is but not what it will do. The purpose of writing a plan of action is to fill that gap, to give the corporate community an idea of where you are going and how you are going to get there. It also becomes the foundation for the annual budget.

Ideally, the long-range goals of the organization (what it wants to accomplish in the next three to five years) will be developed through strategic planning by the board and the staff. If there is not time for that, an interim measure is to develop the goals on the basis of what you are presently doing. If your current programs and activities fit your mission, then you can project what you would like to be doing with each one three to five years hence. This process, of course, does not tell you whether you *should* be performing these current functions; it is based on the *assumption* that all of your programs are appropriate to your mission. Strategic planning is a way of testing your assumptions and is a process that should be undertaken at the first opportunity.

Once the long-range goals have been established, the next step is to outline precisely what you plan to achieve during the current fiscal year toward the accomplishment of these goals. Wherever possible, deadlines and specific, measureable results should be included. Either in the plan or in a separate document, the responsibility for carrying out each aspect of these plans must be assigned.

The three plans of action shown in Exhibit C suggest what your plan of action might look like. Note that each plan begins with the overview followed immediately by the long-range goals and deadlines. All three are kept as brief as possible. Phrases like "wherever feasible" and "such as" make allowances for unanticipated obstacles or environmental changes.

THE BUDGET

The budget and the plan of action must work together, for you cannot determine what money you need and how it will be spent until you decide exactly what you want to do. Conversely, you cannot determine what you *can* do unless you can project what your revenue and expenses will be.

The first step in developing the budget is to determine in detail the requirements—personnel, supplies, facilities, etc.—of your plan of action. Once this has been done, the total costs of these requirements must be estimated both by comparing with the previous year's levels and by building up expense estimates based on the costs of the individual components. For example, if a particular program needs fourteen full-time musicians and two administrators, a certain salary package must be projected. On top of this, rent, supplies, travel expenses and services must be added.

Once the expenses have been outlined, the same process must be used for revenue, including earned income, foundation grants, individual contributions, government aid, and corporate gifts. The revenue figures in your budget will be based on comparisons with last year, realistic estimates as to new revenue sources, and other careful projections. Which sources seem firm? Which do not? How much must be obtained from each income category?

If, as is often the case, revenue is less than expenses, then the plan of action must be reviewed to determine priorities. What is basic? What can be cut back, postponed or dropped? Which programs will you carry out only if you receive full funding for them? Which are so integral to your mission or so complex that you must begin them and hope that adequate funds can be found later? One way or another you must bring your plan of action and your budget together. There is no point in trying to operate at an unsupportable level. That can only bring disaster in the end. (Sample budgets for the David Wilde Dance Foundation and the American Council for the Arts are contained in Exhibit D.)

You have clearly and succinctly described your organization — what it is, what it plans to do — and identified its financial need. These documents form a factual foundation upon which you will build the entire structure of your corporate fund drive.

5

OUTLINING A FUNDRAISING STRATEGY

A corporate fundraising strategy must be an integral part of your organization's overall fundraising effort. You must review the kinds of support that are available, determine those which you need, and identify the potential funding sources most likely to provide that support. You must then determine the type of fundraising campaign that will be most effective for your organization.

FUNDING POSSIBILITIES

There are three major types of contributions an organization can receive from any funding source—general operating support, project support, and capital support.

General operating support is a contribution to support an organization's ongoing functions. Because it is not usually given for a particular project or accomplishment, such unrestricted support gives the recipient maximum flexibility in deciding how it is used. It is also an easy type of support for which to seek renewal in ensuing years because it does not require that new projects be developed to receive continued support from a donor, only that the organization continue to carry out its general programs. Such contributions, if renewed annually, can become an organization's most stable source of support.

However, general operating support is often harder to obtain as an initial gift from corporations than other kinds of assistance. Even though most companies provide some level of operating support, a number of companies are putting increasing emphasis on project support, especially for previously unfunded organizations. It is easy-to-measure, limited, and highly visible. Since operating support is not glamorous, nor is it tied to specific accomplishments, some companies may not respond positively to such an appeal unless they previously have supported one of your projects.

Project support is a contribution to a specific program or activity of an organization. Such support often affords much glamor, visibility and a sense of achievement to the donor. Project support might be given for an ongoing program or service or to support a specific effort to improve an organization. For example, underwriting the development of a marketing campaign or the first year's salary for a development officer could both be considered types of project support.

Although project support may be slightly easier to obtain from a corporation than general operating support, it is not as desirable for the donee. Since such funding is restricted to supporting a specific activity, it provides little flexibility in how it is used; in fact, if the funded project is not completed, the donee may have to return the money. Furthermore, unless the activity is something which can be repeated annually, you will have to develop a new project each year that appeals to the donor in order to continue his support to your organization.

When the funded activity *is* an ongoing program (e.g., an annual series of candlelight concerts), then project support takes on some of the characteristics of operating support. Since one of the organization's ongoing activities is being funded and no special project development is required, this type of support also can be a stable source of revenue.

Capital funding, in a sense, is a special type of project support. In this case, the project is the creation or improvement of an asset which will benefit the organization for a long time. The most obvious type of capital project is for a building—"bricks and mortar." Improvements, such as installing temperature controls in a museum, are capital projects as well. A capital campaign also can be conducted to establish or enlarge an endowment, a fund set up to support ongoing operations or specific activities from its investment income.

Since, by definition, a capital project involves the development of an asset, there are some unusual possibilities for arts groups: choreographing and mounting a new dance or composing a symphony may be construed as capital projects if they are to be used to benefit an organization in years to come. Similar consideration might be given to buying works of art for a museum.

Capital campaigns nearly always focus on developing large assets and are conducted infrequently. While capital campaigns are not specifically discussed in this book, the general principles of corporate fundraising described are applicable.

Within the context of each type of support, you should examine your financial needs, your plan of action and your budget to determine the kinds of support you should seek. As indicated, general operating support is the most stable and flexible type of funding with which to meet your needs. You have already developed the rationale for seeking this kind of contribution by constructing the essential documents.

Capital funding usually should be sought only for major projects which add to your asset base. Generally, a brief review of your plans will determine whether or not there are capital projects for which you should seek support.

To determine your organization's possibilities for project support, you should analyze each of your organization's programs for its appeal to funding sources and develop a specific budget for each. This process should involve only a review and slight refinement of the program analyses that you conducted to create the essential documents.

For example, a theater may have a performance series, a community program, and an in-school performance tour. Each activity might be viewed as a separate project and funding sought for each. In addition, if education and outreach constitute one of the theater's ongoing activities, project funding might be sought to encourage student or senor citizen attendance.

After each possible project is outlined — its purpose, content, impact, budget and potential appeal, the next step is to determine the most probable sources of funding. For which projects should corporate support be sought? Which projects are more likely to be funded by sources other than corporations? A framework for these answers can be created by understanding the characteristics that typify each major funding source.

POTENTIAL FUNDING SOURCES

There are four broad categories of funding sources: foundations, government, individuals and corporations. Although there is much variation within each category, certain observations can be made to help identify the sources of funding which offer the greatest probability for success. Which sources are most likely to support the organization as a whole, which might only support special projects? Which of your projects are most likely to appeal to each type of funder?

Foundations. In general, the primary interest of foundations is project support, especially projects which require a one-time, rather than an annual, contribution. For example, start-up funding for a program which will substantially improve your organization and which can eventually generate self-supporting revenue is a good foundation possibility. Many foundations may also have a special emphasis on areas in which your activities might have an impact, such as minorities, the elderly or specifically the arts. With few exceptions, foundations are interested only in activities that serve the community in which they are located.

Government. Government, or public funding, can be categorized by level—federal, state, county or municipal—each with its particular geographic emphasis.

Usually, government support is given only on a project basis, although the projects may be ongoing programs. Unlike foundations, government support often is not predicated on a short-term, one-time involvement. For government, the essential ingredient is that the project must be seen as important in advancing the goals of a particular agency or the government as a whole. It must be for the public good; must benefit certain special constituencies, such as the elderly or the handicapped; or must help carry out necessary government functions, such as transportation and safety.

Individuals. While difficult to characterize, individual contributors range from large patrons giving thousands of dollars to small donors giving only a few. For the large donor, the amount of support depends largely on the relationship of an individual with an organization — as a board member or founder, as a past trustee or advisor. This is generally true of operating and special projects support; it is especially true of deferred giving (bequests by individuals to your organization), which is an important source of capital support from individuals. The likelihood of getting a substantial amount of gifts from individuals is a direct function of who is involved with your organization.

Corporations. Corporations, like foundations, tend to favor supporting activities and organizations in communities in which they are located. Of the four kinds of funding, this is probably the best source of general operating support.

By reviewing the types of projects you have outlined and the general characteristics of each potential funding source, you should be able to identify which of your activities have a strong possibility of being funded by non-corporate sources. Once this has been done, you should build into your corporate drive the projects that seem to have a high probability of being funded by business. If it is clear from your experience or research that a particular company has a strong preference for project support, you should submit a project proposal to them rather than one for operating support. However, while selected appeals for project support are an important element of your corporate fundraising effort, the main thrust of your strategy should be to seek general operating support.

METHODS OF FUNDRAISING FROM CORPORATIONS

There are two basic methods used to raise money from business. The first is the one-on-one approach, where each company is approached individually. The second is a mass appeal, in which a standard approach is developed and delivered to the business community on a broad scale.

One-on-One. The most effective approach in any fundraising campaign is the tailored solicitation of a prospect by someone he knows well and to whom he will respond positively. In corporate fundraising, the solicitation usually is done by a board representative and a staff member. However, soliciting each prospect one-on-one is very difficult since you will not be able to establish a personal connection with someone who makes contributions decisions in every corporation you approach. Furthermore, one-on-one solicitation is very time-consuming both to set up and to carry out. As a result, direct one-on-one solicitation is usually reserved for prospects who are likely to give large amounts for either project or operating support. Direct solicitation of other prospects during the campaign is encouraged but left to the volunteers to carry out by themselves without staff participation.

Mass campaign. For the very small giver, a mail or telephone campaign may be used since the rewards generally do not warrant the time and effort involved in personal solicitation. The larger the prospective gift, the more personalized the solicitation should be.

Most campaigns use a combination of these two approaches, but the degree to which either one is used in a particular fund drive can vary considerably.

TYPES OF FUND DRIVES

The type of fund drive you implement — the degree to which you conduct a broad, large-scale campaign or a narrowly-focused one — depends upon three factors: the amount of money you need to raise, your fund drive's beneficiaries, and your organization's fundraising history.

Funding Needs. In some respects, corporate fundraising is a "numbers game" — the more money you must raise, the more contributors you need; the more contributors you need, the more prospects you must solicit. Obviously, a few large contributors can offset the need for many small ones, but this is counterbalanced by the fact that it is usually far more difficult to get large contributors than small ones. A good corporate campaign has a range of contributors from large to small. Typically, the top 20% of the donors in a well-developed fund drive contribute 50–80% of the total amount raised; conversely, 80% of the contributors will give only 20–50% of the total dollars (Table 3). Both are needed: the former because of the magnitude of each gift, the latter because they provide a broad base of support, which is both an inducement for the large donors to stay involved and a potential source for future large donors. The number of contributors is an important symbol of the credibility and importance of your efforts. The larger your funding requirements, the more broad-based and intensive your campaign must be.

Beneficiaries. Essentially, the fund drive will be conducted to raise money for your organization or to raise money for a number of organizations (your own included). The largest of the latter type of campaign include the United Way and Combined Health Appeal in the social services and health fields and the local united arts fund in the arts field. These fund drives are communitywide, they are conducted on a large scale, and their proceeds are distributed among a number of benficiaries. Multiple-beneficiary campaigns must be broad-based, not just because they generally require large amounts of money, but because they usually have been developed and sold as appeals on behalf of a number of agencies which benefit the community as a whole, or a large part of it. They must have a communitywide image and impact.[3]

A campaign for a single organization, however, may not make such claims and may seek only to raise money from a relatively small-scale, limited appeal. The size of a single organization's campaign is important more for what it can raise than for the image it connotes.

Fundraising history. If your organization has had considerable

---

[3] Here, and throughout the text, the discussion has been limited, for purposes of simplicity, to an "organizational campaign"—typifying a small-scale, limited corporate fund drive —and the "communitywide campaign"—characterized as a large-scale, broad-based effort. Most drives will, in actuality, contain elements of both.

TABLE 3

AN ANALYSIS OF CAMPAIGN RESULTS

Sample Organizational Campaign
1. Total Raised $210,800
2. Breakdown

10 largest companies	$112,500	(53.4%)
74 other companies	98,300	(46.6%)
Total	$210,800	(100%)

Sample Communitywide Drive
1. Total Raised $625,000
2. Breakdown of Gifts

GIFT SIZE RANGE	NO. COMPANIES
0 – $ 100	450
100 – 250	224
250 – 1,000	69
1,000 – 2,500	29
2,500 – 10,000	21
10,000 & over	12
Total	805

3. Breakdown of Dollars

Top 12 companies	$407,500	(65.2%)
Other 793 companies	217,500	(34.8%)
Total	$625,000	(100%)

success in the corporate fundraising area, then it can conduct a more sophisticated and widespread campaign than an organization which has never conducted a corporate drive. In the case of the latter, if at all possible, you should not create a large campaign that *might* succeed but develop a limited campaign that *will* succeed — that will provide good experience and a solid base from which to launch next year's efforts. It is important in fundraising to do a few things well rather than many things poorly.

THE STRATEGY OUTLINE

With all of the preceding in mind, you can now develop an outline of your basic corporate fundraising strategy by systematically completing each of the following steps:

Step 1. Analyze your programs and the general preferences of various funding sources to determine which of your activities are most likely to appeal to corporate funders.

Step 2. While your corporate campaign typically will focus on soliciting general operating support, you should analyze the giving patterns of selected companies to determine if it is best to use a project approach instead, particularly if they have not supported a general appeal in the past. Special one-on-one approaches should be made to selected companies for major gifts — either for general operating support or for special project support.

Step 3. If you need a large amount of corporate support, conduct some type of federated or united fund drive, and have had a good fundraising history, your basic strategy should be based on a corporate campaign that is communitywide, large, and highly sophisticated. At the other extreme, if you do not need much support, are raising money only for yourself, and have no corporate fundraising history, then your campaign should be very limited — probably carried out by just you and selected board members.

By completing this strategic outline, you have determined the kind of campaign you would like to conduct. You must now determine whether or not your plans are feasible.

6

DETERMINING THE SCOPE
OF THE FUND DRIVE

Once you have outlined a corporate fundraising strategy, you must determine the fundraising effort required to meet your budget and carry out your plans.

There are three steps involved in determining how large the scope of your fund drive can be: developing a list of prospects, evaluating the prospects' giving potential, and arriving at a realistic campaign goal. As with many other phases of a corporate drive, each step is partially dependent on the other steps. For example, the amount of money you need to raise in part determines the size of the prospect list. However, if your organization will be unable to solicit that number of prospects effectively, you may have to lower your goal and make an adjustment in your budget. Thus, each step must be outlined, its impact determined, and then reviewed in light of the requirements and ramifications of each other step.

DEVELOPING THE PROSPECT LIST

To develop a list of potential donors, you must first determine the parameters within which companies will be considered prospects and then identify the companies that fall within those parameters by researching available sources of information.

In seeking new names for your prospect list, there are three basic parameters to keep in mind: geographic area, prospect type, and list size.

Geographic Area. Generally, you should confine your prospect list to companies that have operations in the geographic area you serve. Not only are they more likely to know of your activities, but also, as discussed in Chapter 2, one of the most important criteria companies use in evaluating requests is the potential impact of a gift on the company's local community. Unless you can demonstrate that you are serving the areas in which a company is interested, you will have a difficult time getting a contribution.

Your current geographic area can be ascertained by surveying the residences of your core audience as well as those of the broader audiences served by your touring programs. If a major company is located in a town adjacent to your service area, you might want to make a concentrated effort to service that town in order to solicit the corporation — provided, of course, such an expansion would be beneficial to the new constituency, would fit within your mission, and would not strain your resources. A broad geographic area encompasses more firms and potentially can yield more dollars than a small area, but it also requires more solicitors, more coordination, and more complex logistics. A balance must be sought between the costs and benefits of such an expansion.

Prospect Type. All types of companies should be *considered* as potential prospects, but only those most likely to give should be *selected* to be part of your current prospect list. Given sufficient time and resources, you should develop and analyze a comprehensive listing of *all* firms in your area — manufacturing, financial, retail, service, professional (law, medical, accounting, etc.) — then add to your active prospect list those of the type and size most likely to give. For example, if 50% of your current donors — or companies involved in some way with your organization — are financial institutions, then the chances are good that similar firms which have not yet contributed can be persuaded to do so. Not only do your programs appear to have a particular appeal to such companies, but the example of those currently involved will be an inducement for others to join as well. Furthermore, executives recruited as solicitors from your list of current donors may feel most comfortable approaching their peers in similar institutions.

Certain companies may be good prospects because of the nature of their business. Service institutions may want to increase their name recognition, for example, and retail stores their visibility. Add some of these "unknowns" to your list as a test, with the balance to be added next year if this pilot effort proves successful.

If there is neither the time nor the resources to develop a complete list from the top down — by developing a comprehensive listing of all the business firms in your area and selecting the good prospects — then work from the bottom up. Take your core list — those currently involved plus referrals — and add to it those types of businesses which, by extrapolation from the core list, seem the most likely prospects and about which you can easily obtain information. If your current contributors include a number of financial institutions, for example, you should obtain a list of all the banks, insurance companies, and related businesses in your area, and add them to your list. You can take the more comprehensive approach next year, when you have additional experience and planning time.

List Size. The larger the prospect list, the more solicitors will be required, and the more work will be involved in mailing, record-keeping, and other routine activities. The most serious danger in preparing the list is failure to take into account the practical limitations of time, personnel and other resources required for the campaign.

The best way to avoid the danger of excessive expansion is to set a time limit for the preparation of the list and a numerical limit on its size. Ideally, the basic list should be completed six months prior to the beginning of the campaign. The target number of prospects to be established depends not only on the size of the current list but also on the projected number of solicitors. As will be discussed later, each solicitor should be assigned no more than five prospects; thus, a minimum of ten solicitors must be recruited for every fifty prospects added to the list.

Sources of Names. The core of your prospect list is the group of companies who are already involved with your organization.

Current donors are obviously the first firms that should be considered. In addition — or if there are no current donors — you should consider companies with other degrees of involvement. For example, corporations represented on your board are primary prospects; a trustee's involvement in your activities and his commitment to your efforts provide a strong incentive for him to involve his company in your support. Moreover, an adage among fundraisers states that you really cannot solicit others effectively until you yourself have given.

You should also review each facet of your organization to see where corporations or corporate representatives are involved. Do you have corporate subscribers? Do you use corporate volunteers? Are there corporate advertisers in your programs or corporate donors of in-kind services? A positive answer to any of these questions indicates a source of potential contributors, for they have already demonstrated some interest in your organization and some commitment to it.

The second major source of prospects is referrals. Each of your trustees should be asked if there are companies within which he has contacts or that he knows have a giving program in your area. Each volunteer you recruit, as well as the members of your evaluation committee (described later in this chapter), should be asked for similar recommendations.

Lists of contributors to other organizations, especially those similar to your own, comprise the third major source of potential contributors. Since most arts organizations list their donors in programs and other materials as a form of recognition, such company names are not difficult to obtain. In fact, your own board members may have contributors lists from other organizations with whom they are affiliated.

There are several national directories from which prospective donors in your geographic area can be chosen. All are available in most libraries or may be purchased directly from the publishers:

- *Guide to Corporate Giving in the Arts* (American Council for the Arts, 570 Seventh Avenue, New York, NY 10018) profiles the giving policies and practices of hundreds of companies around the country. This book includes information on: types of activity supported, total dollars contributed and number of gifts, evaluation criteria and application procedures.

- Business directories provide complete listings of companies, including their sales volume, number of employees, products or services, and the names of board members and top executives. Among the most useful are: *Standard & Poor's Register of Corporations, Directors and Executives*, (Standard & Poor's Corporation, 25 Broadway, New York, NY 10004); *Dun & Bradstreet's Million Dollar Directory* (Dun & Bradstreet Corporation, 1 Penn Plaza, New York, NY 10019).

- Local directories or lists of companies in your geographic area can be obtained from your local chamber of commerce, state and local economic development agencies and the departments of commerce and labor. Dun & Bradstreet also has computer lists of businesses in various areas. Even a perusal of the Yellow Pages can be useful in adding to your prospect list.

Prospect Information. Information about each firm should be limited to that which is clearly useful. Excessive data — facts that are "nice to know" but not essential — will only complicate and overburden the system. The basic information is the company's name, address, and telephone number, as well as the name of the person to be contacted (the president, if no one else is specified). Two or three years of the company's contributions history, including names of previous solicitors, is also important.

Certain other facts are useful though not absolutely essential. The Standard Industry Classification (SIC) code number indicates a particular company's type of business. This can be obtained from business directories or from the federal government's Standard Industrial Classification Manual. Measures of business volume, such as total sales and number of employees, can also be useful. These figures, together with the SIC code, can serve as the basis for making comparative evaluations among firms.

After the prospect list has been compiled, the name, address, telephone number, and contact's name must be verified by telephone for each company. Misspelled names or wrong phone numbers frustrate and annoy both prospect and solicitor and will hamper the entire fundraising effort. The verification process should begin three months before the kickoff. On average, 40 such telephone calls can be made in an eight-hour day.

The information about each prospect should be compiled and kept in an orderly fashion (see Chapter 11). If the list size exceeds several hundred companies, substantial time savings can be realized by keeping the information on a word processor or computer. Exhibit E shows a sample format for a computerized prospect list.

PROSPECT EVALUATION

One of a campaign's most critical aspects is determining how much money to ask each company to contribute. Too low a determination will result in getting less money than possible; too high a determination will lead to unrealistic expectations for the total goal. An excessively high request may even so affront a prospect that the company will give little or nothing. The circumstances of a company, its specific philosophy and the involvement of the company's executives in your efforts are the critical factors in determining the size of your request. By carefully evaluating these factors, you should be able to determine the maximum gift size or gift increase that can be requested and a justification for doing so that will appear reasonable to the prospect.

The Evaluation Committee. Although for a small organizational drive your board's corporate fund-drive committee will usually make the prospect evaluations, for larger drives it may be useful to form a separate evaluation committee of five to ten members, some of whom may be drawn from your board, others recruited from outside. The evaluation committee should include previous solicitors, business executives (especially bankers), and individuals from a variety of fields with an in-depth knowledge of the community and local business. These individuals need not be the top community or business leaders, but they must be knowledgeable and willing to put in the required effort.

As soon as the prospect list has been drawn up, the evaluation committee should meet to review the names on the list and determine the amount to be asked of each. To give members a sense of importance and to make sure they attend, the meeting should be hosted by your fund-drive chairman or vice-chairman. If you have a large list of prospects, you can make the committee's task manageable by confining their review process to the top several hundred companies, which you can select in advance on the basis of sales volume or number of employees. Companies which do not meet whatever criteria you set can be evaluated by you and your staff or else assigned an arbitrary amount, such as $100. Because these small companies will probably not give very much, there is little risk if an evaluation is wrong. Thus, your strongest efforts can be focused on larger donors, where a wrong judgment could seriously damage your overall goal.

Depending on the committee and the list, a good rule of thumb is that one hour of committee time will be needed for every 30–40 companies to be reviewed. The committee assembles around a table with each member having a copy of the list before him. One by one, the companies are evaluated according to giving potential, contact, possible solicitor, and pertinent background information. You and another staff member should take detailed notes.

Evaluation Techniques. The prospect evaluation process is essentially a system of educated guesswork, based in part on two factors: comparison and history. These factors are important because they are used by corporate contributions personnel to evaluate requests. Two of the most frequently asked questions in the internal contributions process are: "What did we give before?" and "What are other companies giving?"

With prospects who have contributed previously, a review of their giving history will provide the best clue to what they might consider giving in the future. A history of substantial increases suggests that another one might be requested. Five years at the same level could be used to justify an increase, since costs have risen and your programs may have expanded. A large increase the previous year may mean that this year you should ask for a minimal increase

— or none at all — so that the company does not feel that any large increase it makes will condemn it to an endless series of ever-larger upward leaps.

If a company has not given to you previously, you may be able to obtain figures on its giving in other areas. ACA's *Guide to Corporate Giving* provides some basic data on the corporations it covers. Information may also be obtained from other charitable institutions in your area. These figures can then be used as a basis for your own request from a particular company.

The exact size of the increase will also depend on the campaign's increase. If your overall goal increases only five percent from one year to the next, a company may well balk at a request to increase its gift by 20%.

One of the most effective techniques for gaining an extraordinary increase from a company is the appropriate use of comparisons. If a company's giving level is well below that of its peers in the community or in its industry, it can often be induced to make a substantial increase. Comparison is one of the factors most frequently employed by contributions officers to determine what they will give to a particular cause. In many instances, their comparison is roughly based on sales volume, assets, and number of employees. Thus, their tendency will be to give according to certain ratios: "Our sales volume last year was about 80% of the Smith Company's. If they give $5,000 then our gift should be roughly $4,000." Exceptions may be made to these guide lines if there is a special corporate or executive interest in a particular cause. If a company's president is chairing the hospital's annual campaign, for example, that company's gift will probably be much larger than the rule of proportions would normally dictate.

Experienced fundraisers in a community will know these ratios; so will many corporate executives, especially the contributions officers. Involving such people in your campaign strategy and evaluation process can be very important.

Directories may provide further information on typical levels of giving for companies of a particular industry. This can be important, since companies often base their giving on comparisons with what other companies in the same industry are doing.

This is definitely true of large companies and may also be true of smaller companies as well. Banks, for example, may be induced to increase their giving if they know that their peers in similar communities are contributing at a much higher level. Although comprehensive information in this area is difficult to obtain, *Guide to Corporate Giving* may provide some of it; exchanges with your fundraising peers in other communities are usually the best source.

As a variation on the comparison theme, many companies will gauge their gifts by the size of your campaign goal. It may be their policy not to give more than 10% of any drive's total goal, a consideration often based on their analysis of what their role with respect to other contributors in a campaign should be.

Again, all prospect evaluation is essentially guesswork, but your educated guesses must be based on careful consideration of the above factors. Only with this kind of thorough research and analysis can you be confident that every target is realistic—a critical consideration since, as will be seen in the next section, the determination of your overall campaign goal is based on the sum of these evaluations. A reasonable, well-justified evaluation also constitutes a very persuasive argument as to why a prospect should become a contributor, or a current contributor should give at a higher level.

Prospect Analysis. Once the evaluation process is complete, companies should be sorted by dollar amounts to determine the key prospects—those in the top 10–20% will usually provide 50–80% of the total dollars raised. These companies should be approached in a separate and special manner, as Chapter 9 will outline. Sorting the evaluations by SIC code will determine the relative importance of various industries and whether or not they also warrant a special approach.

SETTING THE CAMPAIGN GOAL

The official dollar goal for your campaign is an important figure. Too low a goal provides too little incentive; too high a goal will dampen the enthusiasm of your volunteers and make them feel they are being asked to work too hard to reach a goal they "know" they can't achieve. And failure to reach the target could have a negative impact long after the close of the campaign by limiting your ability to recruit volunteers for future drives. People want to be part of a winning team; they want their efforts to produce success. When you announce your official goal, you are setting the measure of your campaign's success — or its failure. This figure must be a balance between the financial needs of your organization and a realistic estimate of how much money you and your volunteers are capable of raising.

One systematic method of estimating what you can reasonably expect to raise involves breaking down the evaluation committee's target figures into categories — renewals, increases, and new prospects — and assigning a different probability factor to each kind of gift. The probability factors are your overall estimates of probable success with all the companies in each category. They are numerical representations of your educated guesswork and not scientifically precise calculations. If, for example, you feel that "almost all" of the companies currently giving will give again, you might assign a probability factor of 90%. "A few" might be represented by 10% to 15%. The percentages are not meant to be absolutely precise. What is important is that you try to quantify your instincts and assumptions and to establish ranges of giving.

Probability factors which have proven reliable in a variety of campaigns are shown below. In each case, these factors apply not to individual companies but to entire categories of prospects, thus taking into account overestimates for some firms and pleasant surprises for others. These factors should be modified, of course, according to your own experience and instincts.

- Past contributors, taken as a whole, can be expected to give a total of 95% of the total amount they gave the previous year.
- The probability of obtaining the full amount of *all* the increases requested from *all* past givers is 40%.
- The chance of getting your *full* request from *all* new prospects is 15%.

Applying these factors, the total amount that you can reasonably expect to raise in a campaign may be calculated according to the following formula:

Probability Formula

CATEGORY	BASE FIGURE		PROBABILITY FACTOR		EXPECTED AMOUNT
Renewals	(Total amount raised last year)	×	95%	=	$
Increases	(Sum of evaluation committee's target amounts for all past donors, minus total raised last year)	×	40%	=	$
New Prospects	(Sum of target amounts for all companies which did not give last year)	×	15%	=	$
				+	_____
			TOTAL	=	$

Depending on whatever special circumstances may surround your campaign, the total from all categories can be rounded upwards or downwards to arrive at your final estimate of what you expect to raise. The critical assumptions underlying this method are that the evaluation committee has been careful to provide you with realistic targets which on the whole are neither too conservative nor too liberal; that your probability factors are reasonably accurate; and that you have adjusted your final estimate to reflect any special circumstances.

Once you have arrived at a final estimate, you must compare this figure with your organization's budget and close whatever gap may exist between the two figures. This will give you your official campaign goal. For example:

If your organization raised $50,000 last year; if the evaluation committee, after examining each past donor's gift size, estimated the total that should be asked of all these companies is $60,000; and if the sum of the evaluation committee's individual estimates for all the new companies on your list is $80,000; then the total amount to be expected may be calculated as follows:

Past Donors:

Base:	$50,000 × 95%	=	$ 47,500
Increase:	($60,000 less $50,000) × 40%	=	4,000

New Prospects:

	$80,000 × 15%	=	12,000
		Total:	$ 63,000

If the campaign is fairly new, or if there are special cautionary circumstances, you may want to lower the estimate to $55,000. If you feel the figure is too conservative, you may want to raise the total to $65,000.

If the total financial needs determined in your plan of action and budget are $75,000, you will need to review both your plan/budget and the scope of your campaign. Can you categorize your financial needs according to priorities so that your overall operation will not be crippled if you raise only $65,000? Are there companies from which you can ask larger increases? Can you expand the scope of your campaign to include more prospects?

The specific measures you take to bring your expectations and your needs into balance will depend on your individual situation and a thorough review of all your options. Once the official goal is set, you can begin to organize your campaign.

7

ORGANIZATION

The degree of organizational complexity required to carry out a fund drive depends primarily upon the size and the strategy of the fundraising effort. The greater the number of potential contributors, the greater the number of volunteers required to solicit them effectively and, consequently, the more formal and complex the organization must be. If, for example, you are soliciting only 100 companies, the efforts of your board alone should be sufficient to carry out the fund drive. On the other hand, if you are soliciting 1,000 companies, you will need to engage a number of volunteers in addition to board members; layers of responsibility and chains of command will have to be established if the campaign is to be conducted effectively. Generally, the most complex type of organization is required by a communitywide appeal, such as a united arts fund drive or the United Way, where thousands of companies may be solicited. In the case of a single organization raising funds exclusively for its own programs and activities, a much simpler type of organization will usually be sufficient.

Strategy, or the approach used to solicit potential contributors, is another important consideration in the process of determining how your drive must be organized. And strategy is determined, case by case, by the size of the potential gift. The basic principle involved here is that the larger the potential gift, the more personal and tailored the approach should be. The top contributors will be solicited, whenever possible, by a personal call on the part of an influential board member accompanied by the executive director of the organization. The smallest potential donor, who may give $25 or less, may be solicited by direct mail. Those in between these two extremes will be handled by volunteers with personal calls, letters, or by telephone.

For purposes of simplicity, the discussion in this chapter will focus on two types of campaigns: the organizational fund drive, conducted by a single organization to meet its own financial needs, and the communitywide drive, frequently a joint appeal conducted on behalf of several organizations and carried out on a large scale with thousands of prospects and hundreds of solicitors.

BOARD INVOLVEMENT

In both kinds of fund drives it is very useful if your board is composed of individuals who are business executives with some corporate contacts or individuals who can enlist such executives in your cause. The board — directly or indirectly — must open the doors for you, must give you and your organization credibility and influence in the business community.

The board need not consist solely of corporate presidents; upper and middle-level executives may have more time than their superiors and be more willing to commit themselves to fund-raising work. The few business leaders you may be able to enlist as active participants should be used on those corporations with the highest giving potential on your list. If you do not have such leaders on your board, your subscriber and donor lists, as well as referrals by your current trustees, are good sources of candidates.

You may find, however, that recruiting new trustees is not feasible. There are a limited number of leaders whom you can induce to join your board and be active on it. Busy corporate leaders may be reluctant to make such a demanding, long-term commitment; you may simply not have the time to identify and pursue candidates. In such a situation, your board may be able to enlist corporate executives to serve on an advisory committee for the fund drive. Securing a corporate fund-drive committee of business leaders not on the board will broaden your range of contacts and will also tend to increase the giving level of those companies represented on the committee. The attractiveness to the prospective committee member is that the commitment is a limited one. You should, however, ask for more than just the use of the member's name; committee members should be expected to have their own companies give at a certain level, to lend their names to the campaign, and to solicit three to five other major companies. An advisory committee can be an effective way to add breadth and power to any campaign, even where the board itself is influential and already taking an active role in fundraising.

Corporate fundraising is not based purely upon having contacts, but using people who know contributions decision-makers does increase your chance of success. A well-designed and calculated fundraising program can easily overcome the disadvantages of not having corporate contacts, but no amount of personal influence can overcome the liabilities of an ineffective program or slipshod organization.

No matter who is on your board, in any kind of fundraising campaign, it is the board which must take the lead. Ideally, all board members should help with the fund drive, at some level or another. Some will have important connections, others will have time. An artist, for example, might add special luster to your appeal if he accompanies you and your fund-drive chairman on several of the most important calls. Whatever the contributions by individual members to the drive, the board as a whole must *feel* responsible for obtaining the needed funds.

STAFF RESPONSIBILITY

Your job is to make sure the board carries out its responsibility; your job is to write letters, to make reminder calls, to set up appointments, to prepare lists of candidates. Not only is this what you are paid to do, but your livelihood is at stake.

In the most successful efforts, no matter what kind of campaign is conducted, the paid staff must do all the work, must provide most of the initiative, and must apply full ingenuity and effort to make sure that the drive is successful. In some cases, a volunteer will actually do what he says he is going to do, when he says he is going to do it. In most cases, however, pressures in both his private and professional life will limit the volunteer's ability to carry out his best intentions. It is the staff's responsibility to keep things on track.

VOLUNTEER RESPONSIBILITY

Measured against his many other interests and obligations — both personal and professional — a volunteer's involvement with your organization will most likely be limited. He may have the best of intentions, as well as a sense of moral obligation to follow through on his commitment to you. But the requirements of job security and a happy home life will come first. You must, therefore, make the best use of whatever resources he can share.

The most valuable resources the volunteer has to offer — why you turned to him in the first place — are his prestige, his influence, and his contacts. He can reach peers in a manner that no staff member can. As one corprate executive talking to another, his endorsement of your work is the endorsement of a peer, whether or not he knows his fellow executive. Therefore, it is the volunteer's job to help you identify prospects and to make the calls. Your job is to make this as easy as possible by handling all the details.

For example, if the volunteer tells you he knows Jaqui Johnson at Smith-Updike, it is your responsibility to find out Ms. Johnson's full name, her title, the official name and address of the company, and Ms. Johnson's direct phone number. You must be absolutely certain of the accuracy of all the information you gather so that the volunteer's energy and influence can be put to best use securing an appointment and making the call. If you waste the volunteer's time on detail work, or if the information you gather is inaccurate or incomplete, you are squandering one of your most valuable resources.

THE ORGANIZATIONAL DRIVE

Because the organizational drive is a relatively small undertaking, the requirements are not elaborate. Essentially, they involve having the board make all the solicitations and the professional staff take care of all the logistics and mechanics.

As a first step, in undertaking the fundraising effort, the board needs to organize. The president or chairman might take on the leadership of the drive himself, although it is better that he not do so since his presidential duties typically require all of the time he can afford to spend with your organization. A more workable alternative is for the president to encourage another board member to assume the chairmanship of the corporate drive. If possible, this individual should be a corporate executive with influence in the business community.

The fund-drive chairman and the board president should appoint a fund-drive committee, a group of five to ten board members who agree to take the lead in carrying out the campaign. The committee will work directly with you in setting strategy, making contributor evaluations, and identifying potential solicitors. Each person on the committee should solicit five to ten corporations himself. In addition, the committee as a whole must make sure that every board member is doing what he can to help with the fund drive.

If it is determined that the fund drive would benefit from an outside advisory committee, your board committee should help you recruit influential individuals from the community. However, in many instances, your board itself may be able to conduct the entire campaign since board members, because of their special relationship to your organization, will be willing to take on larger responsibilities than non-board members. For example, with a twenty-member board, an eight-person fund-drive committee might be able to solicit 50–75 companies, with the other twelve board members taking an average of three companies each. An additional hundred could easily be solicited by the board on the basis of letters. If the campaign cannot be handled by the board alone, volunteer teams should be put together in a modest version of what is required for a communitywide drive.

THE COMMUNITYWIDE DRIVE

Like other fund drives, the communitywide campaign will have a small list of potential donors who will contribute a large share of the total dollars. Each of these prospects requires a careful, tailor-made approach, with the maximum one-on-one influence of the individual solicitors. This phase of the campaign is very similar to the organizational campaign described in the preceding section: board members or their contacts must take the lead in making sure all of these prospects are approached in a proper fashion. For the rest of the campaign, a full-scale organization is needed, as described in the following sections.

Overall Organization. The complexity of the rest of the campaign is a function of its size. Whereas 100 prospects can be handled by board and staff alone, 1500 prospects requires a larger infrastructure. The communitywide campaign must be organized in the classic pyramid structure so that each person has a manageable amount of work and a manageable number of people to oversee.

Working from the bottom up, volunteers are needed to serve as solicitors, the "foot-soldiers" who will make most of the calls. Since the usual result of overloading solicitors is that nothing gets done very well, each solicitor should generally be asked to make no more than five calls. Not only is this a reasonably low number, but it *seems* reasonable, and few people will object or feel they are being asked to overextend themselves.

For maximum effectiveness, solicitors are grouped into teams of five to eight persons, headed by a volunteer captain. This establishes a good unit of responsibility, especially if the captain has done the recruiting. Three to five captains, in turn, may be grouped into divisions. Division leaders may then report to the chairman of the fund-drive committee.

If your campaign is large enough to involve telephone and mail solicitation on a broad scale, you may want to set up separate teams and divisions for these functions.

The purpose of such a large and elaborate organizational structure is to create units of individuals who feel responsible to each other and who can be contacted easily by their team leader. The sense of unity and responsibility is enhanced by setting a dollar goal for each team and division on the same basis as the overall campaign goal. Goals for total numbers of contributors might also be set. As much as possible, each team member and its captain should be made to feel a personal commitment to reaching these goals. If an individual solicitor does not perform, the captain and his team will pick up the extra burden rather than expecting you and your staff to do so.

A steering committee to act as the operating board of the campaign may be formed by including all division leaders plus the board's fund-drive committee. Direct contact with your board may be a strong motivating force for these volunteers, and involving as many people as possible in the campaign management process will encourage their commitment and enthusiasm. This steering committee should meet several times, both before and during the drive, in order to develop overall strategies for implementing the campaign and to determine how to handle difficult prospects and balking solicitors. (Table 4 is an organizational chart for the communitywide structure just described.)

Job Descriptions. If possible, terms of office should be established for such major positions as chairman and division leaders. During much of the first year of a volunteer's term, he is learning about the drive and gaining experience, it is during the second year that he is most effective. Also, two-year terms for campaign leaders will substantially ease your annual recruitment burden.

An order of succession should be established whereby the chairman of the fund drive is succeeded by the vice-chairman. Both positions may be filled exclusively from the board, or in some instances you can open them to volunteers who have served previously as captains and division leaders. The advantage of the latter system is the incentive it provides for your volunteers, especially if you make the fund-drive chairmanship an automatic board seat.

The basic functions of each fund-drive position are briefly outlined below. These outlines should be used to develop full, detailed job descriptions.

I.   **Chairman** — acts as chief executive officer of the fund drive.
  A. Identifies and helps recruit vice chairman.
  B. Helps recruit division leaders and captains.
  C. Provides policy guidance on strategy and structure
      of campaign.
      1. Supervises division leaders.
      2. Contacts captains if necessary.
  D. Provides general leadership and management
      during campaign.
  E. Solicits major contributors.

II. **Vice Chairman** — acts as assistant to Chairman and
     as his successor.
  A. Precampaign.
      1. Heads the evaluation committee.
      2. Evaluates prospects.
      3. Assigns solicitors with aid of captains.
  B. Campaign.
      1. Helps the Chairman with overall management.
      2. Helps solicit major contributors.
      3. Supervises division leaders and captains, as appropriate.

III. **Division Leaders**
  A. Manage a division of 3–5 captains, ensuring the division
      reaches its goal.
  B. Help set campaign policy as members of steering committee.
  C. Hold periodic division meetings to maintain leadership
      and control.
  D. Make reports to Chairman and staff on a timely basis.

IV. **Captains**
  A. Recruit and manage a team of 5–8 solicitors.
  B. Make sure the team goals are met.
  C. Make sure all prospects are solicited.
  D. Hold team meetings before and during campaign.

V.   **Solicitors**
  A. Precampaign
      1. Attend organizational meetings.
      2. Review materials.
      3. Select prospects.
  .B. Campaign
      1. Solicit up to 5 prospects.
      2. Report results and information to captains.

TABLE 4

SAMPLE ORGANIZATION CHART

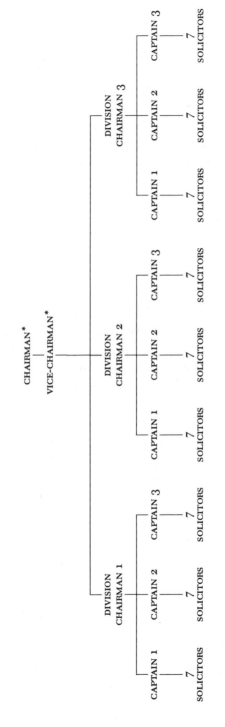

*STEERING COMMITTEE

Volunteer Requirements. The ideal balance for a communitywide drive is a small number of important business leaders — who will solicit a few top prospects and whose reputation will enhance the image of the entire campaign — and a large number of other businessmen, patrons, and community leaders, all of whom will do most of the soliciting.

The best approach to fundraising is direct personal contact. This is done most effectively when the personal approach is by someone who knows either the individual making the contribution or someone within the company who can influence that decision. Businessmen give to their friends and associates, their customers and vendors, and their peers within the industry. As long as the cause is legitimate, important and within the company's guidelines, the imprimatur of a friend or associate is very important. Also, there is often an important *quid pro quo* relationship: Executive A will give to a cause championed by Executive B even though it might not be in Executive A's prime area of interest because A knows he will be approaching B in the next few months on A's major interest. But even if such a relationship does not exist, your volunteer can have some influence merely because he is a member of the corporate community and is, in that respect, a peer.

Given these fundamental principles, the kind of volunteer you want is determined by the types of businesses on the prospect list. If all of your prospects are retail enterprises, then you want your volunteer cadre to be composed primarily of retail representatives, customers, major suppliers, and bankers. It is especially good to have representatives from the most important types of businesses on your prospect list serve on your advisory committee or in other leadership positions. The converse of this principle is true: Volunteers will suggest that prospects with whom they may have influence be added to the list; if you have all retail solicitors, they will provide a large number of retail-related prospects.

Not all of your solicitors need to be businessmen. Any volunteer with influence in the business community is welcome. However, since this is a business fund-drive, it is probable that most of your solicitors will be from business.

The number of volunteers you need is determined by the size of the campaign you can manage. In this respect, it is important to remember that although more solicitations may mean more contributions, the bigger your prospect list, the more work is entailed in every single phase of the campaign. If you adhere to a strict "rule of fives" — five prospects per solicitor, five solicitors per captain, five captains per division — then your volunteer requirements, for example, for the following two different sizes of campaigns would be:

	250 PROSPECTS	1500 PROSPECTS
Solicitors	50	300
Captains	10	60
Division Leaders	2	12
Chairman	1	1
Vice Chairman	1	1
	64	374

This means that for the larger campaign you need to work with 374 people, not 64. There will be 374 calls, 374 solicitation kits, 374 sets of letters and enclosures for each mailing. In other words, every single phase of the campaign will be affected by the number of prospects and the number of volunteers required to solicit them. Therefore, you must also determine how many volunteers your staff will be able to support before you establish a firm figure for the prospect list.

Rules of thumb are hard to arrive at due to the variations in the caliber of volunteers, their ties to the organization, the appeal of the organization's campaign, and the base number of current contributors. One guideline is that one staff person working intensively on a full-time basis for eight months can handle a two-month campaign — requiring 250 volunteers — of 1,000 prospects if he is provided with secretarial help plus part-time clerical assistance at the peak of the campaign preparations.

The primary source of names for potential solicitors is your board. Each board member should be asked for five to ten names of possible captains and solicitors. A ten-person board might produce fifty names. From those initial candidates who accept, you might enlist your captains, who, in turn, you could ask to recruit their own five-person teams. Other sources of names include the evaluation committee, solicitors, other volunteers, subscribers and patrons. Current major contributors are also an important source. The use of a corporation's executives will be important to them because they already have made an investment in your efforts. It is important for you, as well, because the investment of a company's executives helps reinforce that contributor's commitment to you.

Inducements. As with many other phases of a fund drive, successfully recruiting solicitors depends on a combination of altruism and self-interest. The nature of your cause and the arguments you have developed for prospective corporate contributors should also appeal to prospective corporate solicitors, to their needs and interests.

A volunteer may become involved because he loves the arts and wants to contribute to their advancement. He may see fundraising as a means of gaining entry to other more prestigious volunteer positions, such as board membership. He may do so because he is a strong supporter of your efforts and because he wants to do something good for his community. Just as importantly, a volunteer may become involved to further his own professional ambitions. In a large corporation, fundraising is a good way for a middle-level executive to gain visibility, especially if top executives of his company are involved in the campaign leadership. Part of your efforts during the campaign should be to reinforce these inducements, since you will want to use as many of the same volunteers as possible from one campaign to another. If a volunteer has done an outstanding job, be sure you let his company president know about it.

Mechanics. It is far better if captains recruit their own solicitors, and division leaders their own captains. This process strengthens the sense of responsibility and commitment each person has. If, however, your campaign is new, or has a reputation for weak organization, then recruiting may be too difficult a task to leave entirely to the volunteers, and you may have to carry it out yourself. In Hartford in 1977, for example, the staff recruited almost all of the 250 solicitors involved in the Greater Hartford Arts Council's fund drive. This figure represented an increase of 1000% from the previous year's base of 25. It was an arduous task for the staff, but necessary to overcome the bad image the previous, poorly organized efforts had created.

Even in such a situation, however, obtaining the "name" individuals to serve in the highest position should be done either by the board of directors or by the fund-drive chairman. For the balance of the positions—usually all the captains and solicitors—the professional staff must do most of the recruiting. An average day may involve more than 40 telephone calls, half of which are never completed because people are not available. In fact, an average of three calls may be required to reach each person. Of those who are contacted, approximately half will usually agree to help with the campaign.

Under less difficult circumstances, the staff's role will be simply to check with the captains and division leaders to make sure they are carrying on their recruiting assignments. You will then supplement their recruitment efforts only as needed. Again, it is more important to you than to your captains that the volunteers be recruited; if they do not get it done, you must.

As suggested earlier, an effective approach to a prospective solicitor involves an appeal to community spirit, an emphatic guarantee that no more than five prospects will be assigned for solicitation, and your assurance that the solicitor will receive all the organizational support and information necessary to do the job in a minimum amount of time. It is also extremely helpful to mention key executives from the person's own firm who are already involved in the campaign.

A brief thank-you note confirming the agreement and conditions should be sent. Once an individual has agreed to take part, if his company's president is involved in your campaign or sits on your board, send him a copy of the thank-you note; this will be good reinforcement for the volunteer.

If you cannot obtain the required number of solicitors, you should reduce the number of prospects accordingly to maintain the ratio of five prospects per solicitor. Reducing the number of prospects will have a minimal financial effect on the campaign if the smallest firms (in terms of their potential donation) are removed from the list. The alternative, increasing the number of prospects per solicitor, is unacceptable, especially since many of these same solicitors will be needed for next year's drive.

Prospect Assignment. Ideally, every solicitor should look over the entire list and pick the prospects he wants to solicit. In a large fundraising campaign, however, such a procedure is impractical because the list is too long. An effective alternative is to assign prospects to specific teams rather than to individual solicitors. The staff goes through the entire prospect list and assigns companies to teams according to the following criteria:

> a past contributor is assigned to a team that includes that company's past solicitor;

> new or old prospects are assigned to teams that include, in the following order of priority: (1) a solicitor identified by the evaluation committee; (2) the company's executive or senior officer; (3) an executive of a firm in the same field; or (4) a solicitor living or working in the same area as the prospective donor.

These criteria increase the probability that each solicitor will find a prospect he is comfortable with; at the same time they allow him the flexibility of not taking a particular prospect, since specific assignments to individuals on the team are not made.

The balance of the prospects can be assigned arbitrarily to each team until its quota of prospects is filled. In making assignments, the staff should be careful that good and bad, new and old prospects are evenly distributed. Too many problems assigned to one team can greatly discourage both the captain and his solicitors.

8

DEVELOPING THE CAMPAIGN MATERIALS

In addition to the essential documents described in Chapter 4, special campaign materials must be developed. Like the essential documents, they must be prepared meticulously with careful attention paid to the characteristics of the market at which they are aimed.

THE OFFICIAL LETTER

The official appeal letter is the most important of these campaign materials, for it summarizes your assets and focuses the contributions officer's attention on the significance of your activities. If it is used to precede a personal call on the corporation or to serve in place of the call, the letter gains added importance as the first or only contact a contributions officer will have with your organization. It is usually sent with a small number of enclosures.

The letter should be short — one page is the ideal length, two pages the maximum. It should be easy to read and *appear* easy to read — it must not appear crowded or dense. It should be both simple and persuasive. It must be individually typed, neat, and error-free. Obviously, it must conform to the stylistic requirements of proper business letter-writing. In essence, it tells the reader why the activities detailed in the enclosures and in the presentation are important.

Table 5 is an example of the official appeal letter used for the American Council for the Arts. Although the language and style are idiosyncratic to the organization and to the individual who developed it, an analysis of each of its components will illustrate the principles inherent in the letter's development and the message each aspect is trying to convey to the prospective donor.

The Letterhead. The stationery is designed to be attractive, simple, and businesslike, of high quality but not too expensive. Printing the board list on the side eliminates the need for including it on a separate enclosure, an important consideration since you should strive to keep the package you send out as brief and simple as possible. If you have an influential board, featuring their names on the letterhead will give the reader an immediate indication of the stature of your organization. The advisory committee and corporate fund leaders might be listed in addition to or instead of the board list for these same reasons.

The Opening Paragraph should address immediately and directly your organization's mission and significance and induce the contributions officer to read the balance of the letter. In the sample letter, the appeal was being made during a time of economic recession and government cutbacks. Rather than ignoring the difficult environment and unprecedented demands on the contributions budget which resulted, the opening sentence confronts the situation directly and attempts to turn it to ACA's advantage by indicating that it is precisely in such difficult times that a company should support ACA.

The balance of this introductory paragraph is drawn from the organization's overview as discussed in Chapter 4. Those aspects of the overview with strong appeal to business are highlighted here with short, bulleted statements and underscoring. Since the entire overview will be presented in the enclosures, the full version does not have to be repeated in the letter. Three is a nice number for a bulleted list, long enough to appear impressive and not so long as to appear overwhelming. There is no strict rule on this, however; depending on the message, two to five items may be best.

In addition to highlighting the key points of the overview, the opening paragraph might also point out aspects of the organization not included in the overview but important to a particular audience. For example, in Table 5, the second and third bulleted items are designed to reinforce the board list on the side and the contributors list enclosed separately. An activity of particular interest to a retail store might be included in a letter to retailers, or the involvement of a constituency of concern to a particular company might be mentioned.

In short, the opening paragraph is designed to summarize your organization's aims and activities for the contributions officer, to help him recognize your importance, and to encourage him to read the rest of your materials.

Paragraph 2. The ensuing paragraphs should add specificity to the broader statements of the first paragraph in a manner understandable and appealing to business. Words such as "unique," "effective, "management" are important; statistics are useful. Above all, the language should be lean and simple, and all claims must be absolutely supportable. The first evidence of exaggeration or false claims will undercut the credibility of the entire piece.

Paragraph 3. The third paragraph of the sample letter in Table 5 illustrates another application of the basic principle that potential problems must be faced directly. You must anticipate objections and address them; they will not disappear. Difficult questions will be asked — not necessarily openly, sometimes only mentally, sometimes by someone on the contributions committee questioning the contributions officer, but they will be asked. You must have effective answers. If a major part of your program will not be acceptable to business, perhaps you should not seek business funds. Your major activities cannot be hidden; you should never apologize for them.

Paragraph 3 of the sample letter describes ACA's action to achieve equitable public support for the arts, actions which could be interpreted as pushing for an increase in government and therefore taxes, not a very appealing program for corporations. This paragraph is designed to diffuse the potential negative impact of this program and to describe it in terms that are understandable. But even more importantly, it is an accurate reflection of ACA's advocacy message and overall thrust: The arts are part of society and should be treated fairly.

September 8

Ms. Anne S. Russell
Executive Vice President
Data Processing Industries, Inc.
502 Fort Morrison Road
Benton, Illinois 60431

Dear Anne:

In a time of limited resources, the need for the American Council for the Arts (ACA) is greater than ever before. Working to improve the management of the arts and their support by all segments of society, ACA is unique:

o It is the only organization working for all the arts, all across the country.

o Its board includes leaders from the arts, from business, and from other segments of society.

o It is the only national arts service organization to receive such broad support from business.

ACA's unique range of services and programs has a widespread impact on arts organizations all around the country:

ACA is America's largest publisher of books for arts leaders (artists, arts managers, and arts trustees).

ACA's _American Arts_ magazine and _ACA Update_ provide critical information to arts professionals and arts supporters.

ACA offers a unique series of management training seminars for arts managers.

In advocacy as well as in all our efforts, our approach is balanced, objective, and professional: Our position with respect to federal funding is not that the arts are exempt somehow from current economic realities, but rather that they should not be cut more than their fair share and that the business community cannot pick up the shortfall.

TABLE 5
SAMPLE OFFICIAL REQUEST LETTER

The best indication of ACA's importance and effectiveness has been the praise received not just in words but in more tangible terms as well: Over the past year, <u>membership increased 50%, American Arts subscriptions went up ten-fold, the number of business contributors increased to nearly eighty, and book sales rose by 27%.</u>

But in order for ACA to continue its services at prices the arts can afford and to help fill the gap caused by the resetting of federal priorities, we need to broaden our support from the corporate sector.

I hope you will join us this year. A contribution of $1,000 would be one of the most cost-effective you could make on behalf of the arts—<u>to help strengthen their management, to help make optimum use of their resources, and to help solidify their support base.</u>

Your support can give ACA an additional boost this year. We have applied to the National Endowment for the Arts for a Challenge Grant, which means that a gift from you will be used to match the grant if it is awarded.

I am enclosing some background materials for your information. We would welcome an opportunity to talk with you in person about our current plans and activities.

Thank you very much.

Sincerely,

Edward M. Block

EMB:lmw
Enclosures

Paragraph 4. As in Paragraph 2, the last paragraph on the first page focuses on what the organization does. But here the emphasis is on the organization's actual accomplishments, the businesslike results of its efforts as tested in the marketplace. In order to conserve space and to vary the format from the first part of the letter, statistics and underlining are used to call the reader's attention to this paragraph.

Paragraph 5. This paragraph is designed to explain why business contributions are needed to help an organization that is so important and doing so well ("If they're so good, why can't they make it on their own?"). Once again, potential objections must be addressed.

Paragraph 6. It is very important that a specific dollar amount or range be requested. In business parlance, you have to "ask for the sale." You have to tell the contributions officer what you want from him. Sometimes, it is useful to reinforce potential peer pressure. ("I hope you will join California Bank and the First San Francisco at the $2,500 level.")

Paragraph 7. Special incentives, such as a challenge grant, can provide additional stimulus.

Paragraph 8. Depending on what kind of follow-up you intend, the last paragraph should ask for an interview, state that you will call for one, or merely point out that the materials are enclosed. If you do promise to call in a few days, you must follow through. According to a number of contributions officers, many organizations adversely affect their chances by not carrying out these commitments. ("If they will not live up to their word in this matter, how can I expect them to in other cases?")

The closing paragraph used here is designed for a situation in which, for a variety of reasons, such as a long history of giving and frequent telephone and personal contact, an official sales call is not necessary, although it would be perfectly acceptable. It is also phrased in such a way that a telephone call requesting an interview would be appropriate but not mandatory.

The Signatory. Wherever possible, the letter should come from the individual on your board or involved in your fund drive who has the most influence with the addressee. In such situations, titles are not important, only the degree of influence. In other situations, where there is no personal contact, the letter should come from the fund-drive chairman.

Enclosures. Only a limited amount of materials should accompany the official approach letter. Contributions officers may receive fifty solicitation packages a day, and including too much in yours may mean that nothing you enclose is read. It may also put your entire proposal in a negative light.

With a letter containing the elements described in Table 5, you should include only your annual report (discussed on page 82), your current budget and your latest contributors list. If an annual report is not available, you should substitute your plan of action along with a programs summary or as many brochures as are needed to provide complete information on your activities.

Your contributors list must be up-to-date and should be available in two formats: a simple, alphabetical list and a breakdown of contributors by giving categories in which companies are listed according to the dollar range in which their gifts fall ($1,000–$2,499, $2,500–$4,999, etc.). Your choice of which format to enclose in each package should be based on the potential impact on the company to which the solicitation is being made. Reviews should be kept to a minimum. Often it is best to provide a summary like that shown in Table 6, along with one copy of one full review.

Usage. Almost every company requires some kind of official, written request. For some contributors, the official letter may be all that is needed or desired. For others, this should be sent in conjunction with an interview or "sales call." In the latter instance, the letter may precede the call, or be left with the contributions officer at the interview, or sent afterwards. The first method gives the contributions officer a chance to review the materials; the second has the advantage of speed; and the third option enables you to tailor your approach according to what you learn

TABLE 6

SAMPLING OF REVIEWS FOR THE
DAVID WILDE DANCE FOUNDATION

"David Wilde is one of the best dancers on the modern dance scene."

The Times

"His choreography is essentially an art of joy—which is one reason why it's so refreshing to behold."

Dancer's Magazine

"David Wilde's choreographic talent is individual, unpredictable, inspired... as a dancer he is, as always, a joy to watch. But as a creator he is even more original and exciting."

International Times

"The raw energy, vitality, freshness and innovation that characterize American creation in general are found in this Company's style."

Herald-Dispatch

"It is tremendously exhilarating to see such technical virtuosity put to such artistic use."

Times-Dispatch

"I always find happiness, warmth, wit, clarity in everything Wilde does."

The Voice

Full copies of reviews from the following areas are also available:

Colorado	Illinois	New York	Virginia
California	Massachusetts	North Carolina	West Virginia
Connecticut	Missouri	New Jersey	Wisconsin
Hawaii	Maryland	Ohio	
Indiana	Nebraska	Pennsylvania	

England, Venezuela, India

during the interview. The best mix of these usage options is described in the next chapter.

Exhibit F contains samples of other approach letters, which were developed to tie in with the essential documents described in Chapter 4.

THE COVER LETTER

In some respects, the strength of the official letter is also its weakness: Its businesslike detail and precision make it impersonal. To offset this problem, each solicitor may be asked to attach a cover letter which is designed to add a personal note and, in so doing, to show that the solicitor is really committed and not just giving token assistance. Table 7 presents two such cover letters. Solicitors are encouraged to adapt them and to add their own personal touches. Wherever possible, cover letters should be typed on personal stationery. In some instances, handwritten notes might be the most effective format.

THE BACK-UP LETTER

Often, more than one person has an influential contact at a particular company. In such cases, the official letter should be sent by one of the solicitors followed by support letters from the others. Which person sends which letter depends on the circumstances: Who has the most influence? What is the corporate protocol? Who feels the most comfortable making the first and primary approach?

Table 8 is a sample back-up letter. Like the personal cover letter, the back-up letter should be written on personal stationery.

THE PROGRESS LETTER

During the course of the fund drive, it is important to keep prospective contributors informed of your progress and recent activities by sending them periodic progress letters. These notes remind prospects of your work and reinforce its significance. Even more importantly, an impressive accomplishment, the receipt of an

Dear Frank:

Because improving the management of the arts and their support is the mission of the American Council for the Arts (ACA), I serve as a member of its board. Because I am convinced ACA's programs will have a significant impact on corporations as well as arts groups, I am writing to ask for your support.

Although I am certainly aware of the current demands on corporate contributions, I would not approach you if I did not think supporting ACA is an excellent and very cost-effective method of helping the arts—to make better use of their resources and to bridge the gap caused by changing federal policies.

Enclosed is our official request letter, outlining our activities. I hope you will join us.

Sincerely,

[signed by solicitor]

Dear Anne:

I enjoyed seeing you and John at the party on Friday. As I may have mentioned to you, I have been serving as President of ACA for the past three months, and my own company has been a strong supporter of this organization. In fact at a time when pressures on corporate giving are greater than ever before, I think there is no better way to have a positive and widespread impact on the arts than by supporting the American Council for the Arts. For a modest investment, you can have a multiplier effect throughout the arts world for the present and in the years to come.

I've taken the liberty of enclosing our official solicitation letter. I hope you will look it over and pass it along to the proper person. Anything you can do to encourage favorable consideration of our request will be greatly appreciated.

Thank you very much,

[signed by solicitor]

TABLE 7

SAMPLE COVER LETTERS

September 19, 19——

Mr. Franklin B. Pitts
Chairman
Data Processing Industries, Inc.
502 Fort Morrison Road
Benton, Illinois 60431

Dear Frank,

My good friend and fellow board member, Ed Block, tells me he has approached Anne Russell about making a contribution to the American Council for the Arts (ACA).

I can testify firsthand that the programs of ACA have been most helpful to our activities here. I certainly would appreciate any encouragement you can give to Anne and your contributions committee to give our request favorable consideration.

I hope you'll have a chance to come to Atlanta soon and visit Tom and me. It's been some time since we have seen you and Mary.

Warm regards,

Elizabeth Smith

TABLE 8

SAMPLE BACK-UP LETTER

award, or the enlistment of new corporate contributors can serve as an important stimulus for a contributions officer to give your request a favorable response. Such information can be contained in an individualized letter, a sample of which is shown in Table 9, or in a standardized memo addressed to "Contributions Officers." It can be sent either by the chairman of the corporate fund drive or by the executive director of the organization.

ANNUAL REPORT

An annual report for your organization can be an important fundraising tool. If designed attractively as both a business report and a brochure, it can contain highlights of your financial reports and summaries of your programs as well as provide visibility for your contributors and your board. Every publicly held company has an annual report; businessmen understand what it is. It can carry in one eight- to twelve-page booklet all the highlights of six brochures and assorted flyers.

Technically, an annual report describes, in both narrative and financial terms, the history of your organization during the most recently completed fiscal year. It may also contain comparisons with past years and projections of future developments. In one booklet the annual report can highlight all of your current activities and thus streamline your fundraising package. Since it will serve as a sales piece as well as an official report, it should be well designed and graphically appealing, with a large number of photographs and charts. It can be produced in any standard size or shape, but it should probably not exceed sixteen pages in length.

Although contents may vary greatly from year to year and from organization to organization, the following is a good, basic format for a twelve-page annual report:

- One page presenting the mission statement
- Five pages outlining the programs
- Two pages containing the board chairman's official annual report (narrative)
- Two pages of financial statements and comparisons (statistical)
- One page listing the board and officers
- One page of contributors

November 1, 19--

Ms. Anne S. Russell
Executive Vice-President
Data Processing Industries, Inc.
502 Fort Morrison Road
Benton, Illinois 60431

Dear Ms. Russell:

I am very pleased to report that we already have four new corporate contributors this year—Aetna Life and Casualty, Knoll International, R.J. Reynolds, and Xerox. Their gifts are especially welcome this year since we have applied for a Challenge Grant from the National Endowment for the Arts, which, if awarded will partially match any new and increased gift we receive.

I hope you will join our growing list of contributors and help us meet this Challenge Grant. Your support this year is very important to us.

Sincerely,

Eugene C. Dorsey
Chairman
Corporate Fund Drive

TABLE 9
SAMPLE PROGRESS LETTER

THE PRESENTATION

An audio-visual presentation of your organization and its activities can be a very effective fundraising tool. Based on the outline developed in Chapter 4, your presentation can be developed as a slide show, if that will be the best way of describing your activities. However, such a presentation is best used for group rather than individual discussions, such as to a contributions committee. Another, less formal, method which can be used for groups as well as one or two individuals is to use a large notebook as a flip chart from which you can speak. Even here, the formality of this kind of approach can inhibit the development of the personal rapport you need to have with your corporate contact. For the typical corporate call, as will be described in the next chapter, a more personal and informal approach should be taken.

SOLICITOR MATERIALS

Since the fund-drive workers are your salesmen, they must be well-equipped to make the sales call. Although they may not use all of the information, looking through it, picking out what they need, and knowing there is more available will provide them with a great deal of confidence about their efforts.

Exhibit G contains sample materials used in a communitywide drive in Hartford.

9

THE CONTRIBUTIONS SALES CALL

The focal point of the entire corporate fundraising effort is the visit to a prospective business donor. This is the "point of sale," your chance to present your case persuasively enough to convince the prospect that he should support your organization.

WHO SHOULD BE CALLED UPON?

Ideally, as previously indicated, a sales call should be made on every prospect in your fund drive, either by a volunteer alone or by a volunteer accompanied by a member of the staff. However, sales calls are time consuming; you must allow two hours for each one, including travel time. Thus, calling on 40 prospects would consume all of your time for two full weeks. Consequently, you must reserve your time and that of your board members and fund drive leaders for sales calls to the most important prospects. (Volunteers should be encouraged to make calls on all of their prospects. In reality, however, only about 20% of the volunteers will do so; another 30% might make an effort to do so; the balance will use telephone calls and letters.) Certainly, you should make official sales calls on your largest potential contributors. But even a non-giver might be worth a visit if the company's support and involvement in your efforts could be influential with a number of other prospects.

The particular circumstances of the company and its giving history will also be factors in determining whether or not a sales call should be made. Regular contributors, especially those currently represented on the board, may need only a letter.

However, past givers who have experienced a changeover in executive leadership or from whom you are seeking an above-average increase should be called upon. The same is true for large current donors whom you have never visited and those whom you have not seen for several years. For others, current contributors whom you have called upon recently as well as those represented on your board, a call may not be necessary. Even in these cases, however, you should make the offer to visit them and let the contributors decide whether they want to accept.

Using the contact names, potential solicitors, and targeted dollar amounts on the prospect list, the staff should make the first analysis of which companies should be seen by the campaign leaders. This analysis should then be reviewed with the leaders in question to verify the need, determine any special circumstances, and decide who should make the call.

WHO SHOULD MAKE THE CALL?

The prospect list should provide information on the volunteer or volunteers who have connections with each important corporation. The most effective call is made by the staff head of the nonprofit organization and the volunteer with the contact. The more important the call, the more important it is that the head of the staff — not the development officer — make the call. The presence of the chief executive gives a clear message to the prospect that the call is important to the organization. It is a message reinforced by the presence of the volunteer, who has taken time from his job to make the visit — especially if the volunteer is a top-level executive.

In most instances, the ideal number of people for a sales call is two: the volunteer and the director. This gives each the chance to observe which points strike responsive chords with the contributions officer and to amplify these points at the first opportunity. Having more than two people present begins to impede inter-personal relationships and may make the contributions officer feel out-numbered and on the defensive. An exception to this general rule of two is the inclusion of the artistic director — if he would be comfortable at the meeting (or feel slighted if not included) and if his presence would contribute positively to the dialogue.

Occasionally the volunteer may feel it is best that he make the call alone; his judgment on that score should be accepted. In other cases it may be virtually impossible to arrange a time when the volunteer with the contact can make the visit. The best alternative is to go with a volunteer who does not have the contact. Despite the lack of a personal connection, the very presence of the volunteer, especially if he is a leader in the community, will impress upon the contributions officer the importance of your efforts. If all else fails, make the call yourself and try to offset this weakened presentation by a letter or telephone call from the volunteer thanking the prospect for seeing you and explaining the circumstances which prevented him from accompanying you.

THE CONTACT

In most instances the person you call upon will be the person with whom your volunteer has the contact. If you have no such contact, yet it is important that the call be made, you should consult a directory such as *Guide to Corporate Giving*. If no listing is available, you should telephone the company to identify the individual in charge of contributions. This is the individual you want to visit, accompanied by your fund-drive chairman, your vice-chairman, or a board member.

MAKING THE ARRANGEMENTS

The ideal method of setting up the appointment is for your volunteer to call his contact, make a date, and then call you with the time. However, because your volunteer is busy, or he feels uncomfortable making the call, or for any number of reasons, this may never happen. The importance of the campaign's success to you means that you must develop alternatives.

One of the best alternatives is to obtain several available times from your volunteer or your volunteer's secretary, then call the contact and say that you are doing so at the suggestion of the volunteer ("Frances Appleton asked that I call you to set up a time when she and I might visit you."). With your volunteer's available dates in front of you, you can set up an appointment with the contributions officer. It is essential that this phone call be made by either the staff head or the development officer, depending on the potential importance of the prospect. Using a secretary will convey a negative message about the seriousness of your intent; moreover, a secretary may be unable to respond adequately to whatever questions or objections your prospect may have.

If for some reason the initial contact can be made only by the volunteer and not the staff, then your efforts are limited to reminding the volunteer of the importance and timeliness of his arranging the appointment.

PREPARATION

Before you visit the prospect, you should research the company's background thoroughly so that you understand as clearly as possible the framework within which he operates and develop an effective approach. Read the sources mentioned previously — *Standard & Poor's*, *Guide to Corporate Giving*, *Dun & Bradstreet* — as well as the company's annual report and the report on its contributions, if one is available. Review the company's history of giving to your organization and to others. Read past correspondence, as well as the company's contributions guidelines, if available. Ask the volunteer for his advice. You should also examine your own records to see how many of the company's employees are involved in your activities.

Based on all this information, you can then tailor the message outlined in the following section to appeal to the prospect. In addition, you should think through and rehearse what your responses will be to such likely questions as: "What is the most important thing you do?" "How do you differ from this other nonprofit corporation?" "What are you really trying to accomplish?" Developing clear, simple answers to such direct questions is very important preparation for the call.

THE MESSAGE

The purpose of your sales call is to convince the corporation's contributions officer that your activities are important enough to merit a contribution. Based on the outline of your organization discussed in Chapter 4, your message should begin with a brief overview of your organization's mission and importance. You should then proceed to a discussion of your basic activities and why you need outside support. You should always end with a summary of what that outside support will help you to achieve. Keeping in mind the general characteristics of business, the specific information you developed in your research should be used during your interview to highlight the relevance of your work to the company.

In preparation for an interview, you should review your outline and rehearse your message until you are comfortable delivering it in an informal and persuasive manner.

MATERIALS

In order to make the most use of the official letter options described in Chapter 8, you may want to send a brief letter confirming the appointment and enclosing your annual report, budget, and contributors list. This information will give the contact a frame of reference for your organization, enable him to prepare for your visit, and give him the opportunity to include someone else in the meeting if he wishes. These advance materials do not lock you into a specific approach, which you may want to adapt to what you learn about the company during the course of the meeting.

You should bring with you and plan to leave with the prospect the following materials:

- Your current plan of action
- Your board list (if not included in the annual report)
- A one-page summary of any reviews you have received or a sample of the materials you produce, whichever is necessary to give the contact some idea of what it is that you do.

In addition, you should bring materials which contain

information you may be asked for but which should not be left unless specifically requested. These include:

- The Internal Revenue Service's letter determining you are exempt from taxes under section 501(c)(3) of the Internal Revenue code
- An outline of your individual programs
- Sample reviews
- An analysis of your budget along functional lines, by total cost per program (e.g., symphony series) as well as line items (e.g., rent)
- A breakdown of your contributors by giving level.

Any further information and materials you may want to bring will depend on your program and your experience with other prospects.

THE CALL

The content and format of the sales call will vary from company to company and will depend on the interpersonal reactions of the individuals involved. You should approach each call with a definite plan of action and an agenda in mind. The underlying principle is that the volunteer has the influence and prestige; you have the knowledge.

An effective approach is for the volunteer to make the introductory comments, to thank the prospect for his time, and to tell briefly why your organization is important to him, why he has taken time from his work schedule to accompany you. By doing this, the volunteer has given the imprimatur to your efforts and spoken of your group in terms his peer, the corporate prospect, can readily accept.

The volunteer then introduces you, the head of the organization's staff. Keeping your outline firmly in mind, you can then deliver your message in a conversational tone—the importance of your efforts, the functions of your organization, your plans. There may be points at which you want the volunteer to interject his comments in order to keep his presence an integral part of the call and to make the presentation less formal, less like a monologue. These interjections should be discussed and perhaps even rehearsed. "Anne, let me interrupt for a moment, because I think this is an important point. . ." This will also encourage the contributions officer to ask questions as you go along, thereby keeping him involved and interested.

The volunteer should close the presentational portion of the call with his own personal summary. "You can see now why this organization is so important. We think it does a lot of good work in this community. That's why I've joined the board, that's why my company is supporting it at the $5,000 level. Our reason for calling on you is to ask you to join us this year and make a gift in the $2,500 to $5,000 range." Usually the contributions officer will respond by saying that he will give your proposal consideration. In addition, he will most often summarize his company's contributions guidelines, process and timetable.

Both you and your volunteer must be aware that a sales call is a performance in the best sense of the word, and it should be conducted accordingly. The prospect's personal sense of your organization is based upon this performance—the way you present yourself and your materials, the degree of commitment and enthusiasm on the part of your volunteer, your success in relating to the prospect's concerns, the care and directness with which you answer his questions. Like all good performers, you must base your timing on the behavior of your audience, in this case the contact. If he is impatient or bored, make your points quickly and without elaboration. If he is interested, take the time to explain. The average call lasts forty-five minutes; the range is from ten minutes to two hours. It is up to you to determine what timing is appropriate for each call.

You must also pay careful attention to what the contributions officer is saying, as well as to what he is not saying. If his words or his silence indicated that your proposal will probably not be funded, did he suggest what might be acceptable? Can you offer a specific project for underwriting rather than looking for operating support? Can you tailor one of your programs to fit his needs? Your adaptability during the interview or in the follow-up may make the difference between getting a contribution and not getting one.

FOLLOW-UP

Your call should be followed by a brief note thanking the prospect for spending time with you. If an official letter has been sent out, the note can come from you. If not, your volunteer should be the signatory to this thank-you note and should attach it to your official solicitation letter, tailored to the company's interests.

As indicated in the previous chapter, during the weeks between your call and the company's decision you should periodically send information on your progress and activities. It may also be appropriate for you or your fund drive chairman to respond to the submission of a special proposal with a telephone call. If, for example, the prospect expresses an interest in a children's program along certain lines and you send him an outline of a special program afterwards, it is in order to call him to see if that was the kind of project he had in mind.

10

IMPLEMENTING THE CORPORATE CAMPAIGN

In a sense, the corporate fund drive is a series of individual sales calls, carefully organized and even more carefully orchestrated to achieve both the optimum use of volunteer time and the greatest possibility for success. As has been indicated in the discussion of campaign organization (Chapter 6), the complexity of a campaign depends on its scale, with a drive for a single organization at one end of the spectrum and a communitywide drive at the other. For the organizational drive, the official campaign may be no more than the general time of year during which most of the corporate calls are made. For the communitywide drive, the campaign is a major event, with a cast of hundreds, an official opening, and a formal closing date.

THE SCHEDULE

Timing. The larger the gift being sought, the more important it is to have the request made at an early point in the company's budget process. Since, as discussed in Chapter 2, most companies develop their contributions budgets in later summer and fall, these months are the best in which to raise funds from corporations. Thus, for an organizational drive, especially one in which contributions of $1,000 or more are being sought, the corporate campaign should be conducted in the fall. For a communitywide drive, however, a fall campaign is difficult, for this is the time when the most established of all community drives, the United Way, carries out its fundraising efforts. Throughout the fall, on a nationwide basis, the United Way has maximum use of publicity outlets, commands the full attention of corporations, and uses most of the available fundraising volunteers. To put your drive in competition with the United Way would be impractical, harmful to both causes, and cause confusion among donors and volunteers alike. It is, therefore, to everyone's best interest to conduct your major organized fund drive during another period, even though fall is the best time to approach companies.

One answer to this dilemma is to conduct your communitywide campaign in two phases. In the fall, you and your volunteer leaders can solicit major corporations on a one-to-one basis with little publicity, reserving another time of the year for the medium and small prospects of the "public" campaign. For large donations, the timing of each individual company's decision-making process is critical, since a major contribution must be written into a company's budget before it is established. Moreover, in a major corporation there is often a formal contributions process which must be followed. For small prospects, on the other hand, the amount may be small enough to be taken from a contingency fund. In addition, the decision-making process may be sufficiently informal that it does not really matter when an approach is made. Often, in a small company, the decision is entirely up to the president or owner, who can hear a request and approve it on the spot, if he so wishes.

Organizational Drive. Unless an organization's campaign is conducted on a broad or communitywide basis, there may be no official beginning or end. The drive starts when the first letters are sent out or the first call is made in the late summer. It ends in the late spring, when the last contribution is received or the goal reached. Because of the considerations mentioned previously, the peak of activity is in the fall, with a tapering off in late November and December, and with only a few calls made in the early spring, to those companies which have first-quarter deadlines.

On the response side, the peak of activity is usually during the first quarter of the calendar year — for those requests which are being considered seriously. Corporations with fall request deadlines will usually complete their budget process for approval by the board at its first meeting of the year. Once that approval has been given, the contributions can be made.

In summary, unless you are planning a large-scale campaign, you should set August 15–September 1 as the target date for beginning your solicitations, bearing in mind that results may not be known until the beginning of the year.

Communitywide Drive. As previously outlined, the solicitation of major corporations in a community drive must be conducted in the fall. In scope this is a small, nonpublic phase; typically, less than twenty companies will be approached. In dollar volume, however, this is the most significant part of the campaign.

Because of the nature of a communitywide drive, there should be a public phase for the corporate campaign, with an official beginning — a "kick-off" meal or event — which generates publicity and, more importantly, brings all of your volunteers together and helps to get them started on the campaign. In this, as in other aspects, the implementation of a communitywide drive focuses on the solicitor more than on the prospect, for its success will hinge primarily on whether the solicitor makes his calls. If he does not, all of your efforts and materials will be meaningless. On the other hand, a solicitor with an effective approach and a close, personal relationship to his contacts can overcome almost any problem, including a prospect's strong reluctance to contribute.

Usually, volunteers will remain enthusiastic and committed to a fundraising effort for only a short, concentrated period. Consequently, the campaign should last no more than two months; the ideal time span is four to six weeks.

Because of seasonal problems, there are relatively few times when a campaign can be held. Summer is bad because of vacations; early fall belongs to the United Way; the period from Thanksgiving to Christmas is lost to holidays. This leaves the first six months of the year. Your own fiscal calendar, other events in the community, and consideration of specific holidays will further limit the options available to you.

Estimating the Schedule. Once an official starting date for a campaign has been chosen, the time necessary for adequate preparation can be established and a schedule constructed by working backwards from the official date. Of course, the time required to carry out certain tasks will vary widely among individuals and organizations, but experience has shown that a rough schedule can be developed on the basis of the following standard time allowances:

	TIME ALLOWED	
TASK	ORGANIZATIONAL	COMMUNITYWIDE
Developing the Essential Documents	1 month	1 month
Developing the Prospect List	1 month	3 months
Recruiting Volunteers	1 month	3 months
Developing the Campaign Materials	1 month	1 month
Preparing for the Campaign	1 month	3 months
Conducting the Major Prospects Campaign	2 months	2 months
Conducting the Public Campaign	—	2 months

These standard periods do not represent the actual amount of full-time, intensive work that must be spent on each particular task, but rather the span of time that must be allowed for the whole task to be completed. Included, for example, are time spent waiting for people to make decisions, the length of time it takes for materials to be printed, and the time which elapses between your submission of a proposal to your board or campaign chairman and your receipt of approval.

In fact, a number of these tasks can be done simultaneously. Table 10 is a standard scheduling graph for both an organizational and a communitywide drive. As this table shows, you should allow seven months from start to finish for an organizational drive and nearly twelve for a communitywide drive. There is some flexibility: The time allowed can be reduced by 15 to 25%, but the result will be a fifty percent increase in the pressure on you and your staff. In truth, your control of time, except in regard to your own actual work and that of your staff, is minimal; a great deal of your time will be spent waiting for other

TABLE 10

STANDARD CAMPAIGN SCHEDULES
Organizational Campaign
(Starting Date: Sept. 1)

	Essential Documents	Prospect List	Volun-teers	Campaign Materials	Major Prospects	Campaign Prep.	Public Campaign
April	X						
May		X					
June			X				
July				X			
Aug.						X	
Sept.					X		
Oct.					X		

Communitywide Drive
(Kick-off: Jan. 15)

	Essential Documents	Prospect List	Volun-teers	Campaign Materials	Major Prospects	Campaign Prep.	Public Campaign
April	X						
May		X					
June		X					
July		X	X				
Aug.			X	X			
Sept.			X				
Oct.					X		
Nov.					X		
Dec.						X	
Jan.						X	X
Feb.							X
March							X

people to respond or make decisions. You must be careful to anticipate this problem and to account for it in your scheduling.

ASSIGNING THE WORKLOAD

Once the basic blocks of time have been set down and a rough schedule of events determined, the next step is to calculate the actual workload the campaign will require and assign responsibilities to various staff members.

The amount of time you should estimate for each task will vary considerably according to the individuals who perform it, their experience and competence; the circumstances and resources of the organization's overall fundraising efforts; and the geographic and economic environment. Table 11 provides time estimates for a 250-company campaign. In contrast to Table 10, these estimates do not include waiting times; rather, they must be put in by the director or development officer in charge of the campaign. Great caution should be exercised in working with these figures. They are personal estimates, not calculated standards. They should serve as starting points for your calculations, not final results. Using them as a base, you must review carefully each task that must be done and make the necessary adjustments. If necessary, many of these tasks can be done more quickly though less thoroughly in order to meet looming deadlines.

Once you have adjusted the time estimates in Table 11 to the demands of your campaign, you should calculate the amount of time needed for each task on the part of your support staff and volunteers. By combining the resultant time requirements with a carefully estimated schedule, you should arrive at a detailed workplan such as that shown in Table 12. This sample page covers only the first two months of a communitywide drive; the balance of the schedule requires five additional pages.

IMPLEMENTATION

For a small organizational drive, implementation requires relatively little effort: Board members are assigned certain prospects,

TABLE 11

BASIC TIME ESTIMATES FOR A
250-CORPORATION ORGANIZATIONAL CAMPAIGN

	DIRECT STAFF TIME (HRS.)
Developing the Essential Documents	
Inventory & Program Analysis	8
Overview & Outline	16
Plan of Action	8
Budget	8
Outlining the Fundraising Strategy	
Developing Projects	16
Determining the History	20
Outlining the Strategy	4
Determining the Scope of the Fund Drive	
Developing the Core Prospect List	24
Developing the New Prospect List	24
Verifying Prospect Information	24
Prospect Evaluation Research	40
Prospect Evaluation	8
Setting the Campaign Goal	2
Organization	
Campaign Leadership (Chairman, Board Committee, Advisory Committee)	16
Recruiting Sixty Volunteers	48
Developing the Campaign Materials	
The Official Letter	24
Other Letters	4
Annual Report	40
Presentation	16
Solicitor Materials	40
The Contributions Sales Call	
The Standard Message	4
Making the Arrangements	1/Call
Preparation	2/Call
The Call	2/Call
Follow-up	½/Call
The Corporate Campaign	
Outlining the Schedule	4
Assigning the Workload	16
Implementation	8 Hrs/Day; 2 Months

TABLE 12

FUND DRIVE SCHEDULE
SAMPLE PAGE

		ALLOCATION OF TIME (HRS). assigned to:			
Week of:	Description	WGB Executive Director	JL Assistant Director	LK/SB Clerical Staff	MSL * Fund-drive Chairman
10/11	Prospect research compilation	2	10	5	—
	Prepare campaign materials	5	30	5	—
	3rd publicity mtg.: Prelim. design & placement sched.	2	4	2	
	Corporate presentation	10	5	—	10
10/18	Corporate sales call	2	—	—	2
	Publicity meeting follow-up	1	4	2	—
	Mail campaign update	1	4	2	—
	Finalize campaign materials	—	5	2	—
10/25	Computer status report	1	—	—	—
	Sustained beneficiary mtg.: review campaign materials	2	3	3	—
	Finalize major fund proposals	—	10	2	—
11/1	Solicitor assignments	2	8	2	—
	Prospect research compilation ends	5	15	5	—
11/8	Solicitor assignments	1	6	2	—
	4th Vice-chmn. meeting	2	3	4	2
11/15	Update prospect list	—	2	3	—
	Solicitor assignments	2	6	2	—
11/22	Update prospect list	—	—	3	—
	4th publicity mtg.: finalize placement schedule	2	4	2	—
11/29	Update prospect list	1	2	3	—
	Complete solic. recruitment and assignment	2	20	5	—
	Total Hours:	43	141	54	15

*Initials of staff and volunteers

and your main task is to see that they carry out these assignments in an effective and timely fashion. In contrast, the community-wide drive, because of its scope and the layers of volunteers, requires substantially more effort and a more complex organization. Because of this complexity, the following sections will focus on the communitywide drive. If yours is an organizational drive, you will need to make adjustments and simplifications.

THE VOLUNTEER TEAM

In a communitywide drive, the team of solicitors is the key unit in the campaign. These teams and their volunteer members will be both the focus of your campaign and the reason for its success or failure.

During the last six weeks before the official launch of the campaign, with all volunteers recruited and assigned to teams, you should help each captain prepare for and schedule a primary meeting with his team members. The purposes of this meeting are to provide solicitors with basic information on your organization and your campaign; to enable solicitors to select prospects from those assigned to their team; and to generate the team spirit which will be so crucial during the public phase of the fund drive.

The team meeting should last no more than an hour and should be conducted in the same general manner as the sales call: the volunteer, in this case the captain, opens and closes the meeting and sets the tone; the staff delivers the message—a formal, audio-visual presentation of the fund drive. After the presentation, the campaign schedule and deadlines should be impressed upon the solicitors, as well as the goals the team is trying to reach. The bulk of the time then will be spent reviewing the list of companies assigned to the team and giving each solicitor a chance to pick his own contacts. Each team member should have a copy of the team list. You can note down the choices, which you should confirm in writing after the meeting.

If they are available, prizes for the team and individual efforts should be mentioned during this meeting. For example, concert series tickets may be awarded to the top fundraising team, or memberships in a local art museum. Prizes may also be awarded to encourage particular directions in fundraising, such as obtaining the largest percentage increase in dollars raised.

If the campaign lasts two months, you should encourage each captain to hold team meetings every other week, with the alternate weeks spent in telephone follow-up. These meetings should include a review of the status of the campaign as a whole. If a particular solicitor is a problem and does not attend, you can set a meeting around his schedule and hold it in his office to ensure his attendance. This kind of procedure may well be necessary since team meetings during the campaign tend to draw those who have done their jobs, rather than those who need an extra push.

THE CAMPAIGN

The Kick-off. The public campaign should open with a brief, well-organized kick-off meeting that lasts an hour or less. As indicated previously, such an event not only marks the official beginning of the drive, the also provides a high degree of motivation and stimulus to the solicitors. The very presence in one room of hundreds of volunteers is an exhilarating experience for everyone involved. It conveys a sense of the potential power and impact of the campaign and demonstrates how each person can contribute to an impressive total.

All solicitors, captains, and other fund-drive workers, board members, representative individuals from arts organizations, and the press should be present. The presence of prominent business executives and dignitaries may provide an added incentive for attendance and publicity, as will an enthusiastic and prestigious keynote speaker.

Solicitations. One useful technique for beginning the solicitation process is to send each prospect a letter describing the campaign and stating that a volunteer will call shortly. Based loosely on the type of official letter described in Chapter 8, the prospect letter should be timed to arrive on the day of the kick-off. (See Exhibit F for samples.) An annual report or brochure may be enclosed. Not only does such a letter begin to make the prospect aware of your campaign, but more importantly, it serves as a "door-opener" for the solicitor, who can begin his sales calls with, "I'm following up on the letter Bud Horowitz, Chairman of Hager Department Stores, recently sent you."

Solicitors. Ideally, solicitors should be contacted by the captain, and captains by division leaders, or the fund-drive chairman, on a weekly or semi-weekly basis. These contacts should be supplemented by telephone calls from the professional staff. Such close monitoring will help overcome a solicitor's inertia, especially if you have warned him in advance of these frequent calls. Note should be made of any solicitors who do not seem to be doing anything or will not return calls. Depending on the strategy you and the steering committee have developed, any solicitor who has not started work after two weeks should be dropped and his prospects reassigned to the rest of his team — unless there was an exceptionally good reason for his temporary lack of action.

Because a volunteer is not being rewarded financially, you must rely upon his personal motivation. The solicitor's sense of responsibility to his team and his captain may be the strongest reinforcement you have; thus, the size of the team, the number and caliber of team meetings, and the relationship between the captain and his team members are all critical factors. Even so, professional and personal situations may intervene and the job does not get done. There are no easy, general solutions to this problem; it must be dealt with each time it arises with patience, ingenuity, and sensitivity to the needs of the particular individual involved.

ENDING THE CAMPAIGN

If at all possible, the campaign should be ended on time, just as it was begun on time. It is important to give solicitors — especially those who may return next year — the understanding that your deadlines are firm, that there really is only a short amount of time to make the calls. This will encourage prompt action, discourage procrastination, and considerably ease the burdens on you.

It is virtually inevitable, however, that some prospects will not have made a decision by the end of the campaign. Board meetings may not have occurred; reassignments among solicitors and other delays may have extended the solicitation period. For these and any number of other reasons, you should allow an extra month after the campaign's end for "mop-up." After that period, unless significant contributions are still pending, the campaign should be shut off and any remaining prospects carried over to next year's drive.

Frequently, a victory celebration is scheduled for the last day of a campaign to make the ending official. The nature and timing of such an affair can serve throughout the campaign as an excellent reminder of the need for quick action.

FOLLOW-UP

After the conclusion of the campaign, the steering committee and captains should meet to review both its strong and weak points and to determine how the campaign might be improved. Updated information about prospects, with suggestions regarding which ones should be removed from the list and which ones added, can be culled from questionnaires distributed among solicitors by their team captains.

11

CAMPAIGN SYSTEMS
AND SUPPORT

Effective and efficient operating systems are crucial to the success of any corporate campaign. These systems enable the professional staff to handle the details and the mechanics of the drive as well as to provide reinforcement to the campaign, its workers and its prospective donors.

RECORDS AND REPORTS

You must have a recordkeeping system to keep track of every campaign detail—who has been contacted, who has pledged a gift, who has refused. Even for a small, organizational fund drive such a system requires considerable time and effort; for a communitywide drive it is a major undertaking. In addition you must be able to use this information to communicate effectively with your board and volunteers.

Master file. All correspondence, including each letter and each note recording a pledge made by telephone, should be filed in a separate fund-drive drawer. To ensure tight control, the master file should be the personal responsibility of a single staff member. Master file data are vital in tracking down the details of a contribution or a contact, especially when research is being done for the following year's fund drive.

Master list. At the heart of the recordkeeping system is the master list, one copy of which is kept as the final authority on all details. This list should be checked and re-checked; its accuracy should be a matter of fanatical concern. As shown in Exhibit E, the master list, in full detail, contains all the pertinent information on each prospect, from address and telephone numbers to giving history and current solicitors. One person and one person only should be responsible for making all updates and adjustments. From this list you must be able: to determine whose pledge is not yet paid; to update company mailing addresses; and to derive complete and accurate information for the following year's campaign.

Master control. Because the master list must contain all necessary details, it is too voluminous and cumbersome to use on a daily basis. Consequently, a master control sheet, like that shown in Table 13, is required for efficient campaign management. Kept alphabetically with abbreviated entries, it can be consulted at any time for the exact status of any prospect. For a communitywide drive, a printout showing similar information on a one-line-per-prospect basis may be most useful when sorted out by teams. You can send a copy of each team's page to its captain for easy review of his team's progress on a regular basis.

Since this list is only as good as the accuracy and timeliness of its information, keeping the master control list up-to-date and precise is essential. It should be checked frequently for errors.

Status Sheet. Even the master control list can be too detailed if you want to know where the overall campaign is and how you compare with last year. Certainly, it is far too detailed to be given to board members. Summary status sheets, like the example shown in Table 14, are an essential means of keeping others—and yourself—informed of the overall progress of the campaign. At the height of a large campaign, these status sheets should be prepared semi-weekly. For smaller, less active campaigns they can be prepared less frequently.

LETTERS

Acknowledgements. Every gift must be acknowledged with a thank-you letter—an individual one for the major donors and a standard, printed one for the smaller gifts (see Table 15). *People* give to people, and they like to be thanked.

COMPANY	SOLICITORS #1	#2	BACK-UP SOLICITORS	LAST YEAR	DATE[1]	C[2]	CURRENT YEAR AM'T REQ.	SUBMITTED	RESPONSE[3]	FOLLOW-UP[4]

[1]Date: Deadline for request
[2]C: Code indicating type of appeal (e.g. new or renewal)
[3]Response: enter $ amount or "no"
[4]Follow-up: notes date of any follow-up letter(s).

TABLE 14

SAMPLE STATUS SHEET
(Communitywide Drive)

FUND DRIVE STATUS REPORT
AS OF MARCH 1

| | Last Year | | Current Year | | | |
| | Actual | | Total of Evaluations | | Actual to Date | |
Category	No.	Amount	No.	Amount	No.	Amount
Top 15 Companies	15	$413,300	15	471,000	14	450,620
Past Contributors	597	138,318	577	166,840	430	146,300
New Prospects	—	—	990	129,725	221	19,300
Total	612	551,618	1,580	767,565	655	616,220

Goal   **$625,000**

REFUSALS

Category	No.
Top	0
Old	51
New	393
Total	444

Refusals. Despite all of your efforts, some people will refuse to give. In fact, the converse of the success probabilities mentioned in Chapter 6 is that *most* new prospects will not give, and only a few will give at the level requested. In every case you should accept the response gracefully and try to understand why the prospect has not given as you had hoped. Would a project proposal be more attractive than a request for operating support? Was the approach made by the wrong person? Did the company indeed have a bad year?

It has been said that people do not refuse to give, they only defer it; there are times and ways and techniques, which if used, can often change a refuser into a contributor — but not always. However, if you have been unsuccessful with a particular client for three years, then it is time to drop him from the list. Time and effort — yours, your staff's and that of your volunteers — are better spent elsewhere.

Even so, you should respond to every refusal. In the case of a company which has advised you directly that it will not be giving, a letter can be sent expressing your understanding of the situation and raising the possibility of support in another way — through program sponsorship or a donation of in-kind services. A follow-up telephone call might also be useful. If word of a company's refusal has reached you through a solicitor, a letter such as that shown in Table 16 might be appropriate. In either case, mentioning some of the contributors who recently joined your list or describing a new accomplishment of yours may be just enough to change the refuser's mind. It is worth a try.

Volunteer letters. At the conclusion of the campaign, or as soon as his assignment has been completed, each volunteer should receive a special thank-you letter from the president or the fund-drive chairman. Such expressions of appreciation may be the only reward a volunteer is seeking.

PUBLICITY AND PROMOTION

In a corporate campaign, your publicity efforts should be aimed at two audiences: the business community and your solicitors.

AMERICAN COUNCIL FOR THE ARTS

570 Seventh Avenue
New York, New York 10018
212 354-6655
WORKING FOR ALL THE ARTS
NATIONALLY SINCE 1960

February 17

Ms. Anne S. Russell
Executive Vice President
Data Processing Industries, Inc.
502 Fort Morrison Road
Benton, Illinois 60431

Dear Ms. Russell:

Thank you very much for your contribution of $1,000; it will be used to continue our important programs and services for all the arts.

Your support this year may give ACA an additional advantage. We have applied to the National Endowment for the Arts for a Challenge Grant, which means that your gift will be used to match the grant if it is awarded.

Unless we hear otherwise from you, we will automatically list you as a contributor in our publications catalogue, our books, <u>American Arts</u> magazine, and at our benefit and conferences.

Again, thank you very much.

Sincerely,

W. Grant Brownrigg
Director

WGB/km

Mrs. Esther Madison
President
Fortune Corporation
Box 328   WON'T YOU RECONSIDER?
East Weston, Arizona 90153

Dear Mrs. Madison,

One of our volunteers has reported that you did not choose to
contribute to our fund drive this year.

Won't you reconsider? Even a small gift will help the arts and will
be important evidence of your support for them and what they're
contributing to the community.

To give you an idea of the richness and diversity of our program,
we are enclosing a free copy of our new Arts Directory, showing
the more than 100 arts groups in the area.

We hope this directory—and our second appeal—will change your
mind.

Please help us; we need your support. Send in your tax-deductible
contribution today.

Thank you.

Sincerely,

James A. Stewart
Fund Drive Chairman

P.S. Whether you change your mind or not, please keep the
      enclosed directory. You may find it useful in recruiting new
      employees, discovering new things to do, or telling others
      about the area in which you live.

Publicity and promotion alert small businesses and the general corporate community to your activities and importance, and thereby reduce the initial barrier of ignorance that solicitors must overcome before they can make effective presentations. Publicity also encourages the individual solicitor in his efforts by reminding him that he is working for an important cause, which helps motivate him to make his sales calls and turn in his reports. If for example, on his way home from work he must drive past a billboard proclaiming your fund drive, he will receive a daily stimulus to get his job done. For maximum impact, publicity should continue throughout the year, with an increase in intensity during the official campaign.

Often local businesses will donate such items as the presentation of publicity materials and the airing of public service announcements. In addition to the standard media, there are several good publicity vehicles which can be used at little or no cost. Thirty to sixty days of billboard space, for example, can often be obtained for a short message about your campaign. Space in company newsletters may be available for features on employee involvement in your efforts. Speeches before chambers of commerce, Rotary Clubs, and similar associations can be a very effective means of delivering your message to the business community on a periodic basis throughout the year. Your board members and volunteers can provide you with helpful information on how to take advantage of these and other outlets.

REINFORCEMENT

In addition to ongoing publicity, there are a number of techniques which can be used throughout the year to remind both contributors and solicitors of your activities and to reinforce positive feelings about your organization.

Recognition. Because image and recognition are so important to many corporations, you should list your contributors in all of your publications, including your annual report and brochures. This is simply another way of thanking them for their support.

Patronage. Lists of all contributors should be drawn up, both alphabetically and by type of business. These should be sent to all fund-drive workers and board members with the suggestion that the next time they do business with a contributor they express their gratitude for his support of your organization.

Benefits. Special invitations to and priviledged seating at special events are also effective ways of showing appreciation to both contributors and solicitors.

Support letters. Those who benefit most from your services should be encouraged to write directly to top contributors and fund-drive workers to express their appreciation.

Communication. The critical aspect of the reinforcement process is continued communication. Throughout the year, contributors and solicitors should be informed of your special activities and accomplishments. For example, a month or so after the campaign's conclusion, details on the total contributions raised and how they have been distributed should be sent out to all supporters. Releases on special awards and copies of brochures in which you give your donors recognition should also be sent out.

Periodic Visits. One of the most effective techniques to reinforce your campaign activities with contributions officers is to involve them on a personal basis during the months when you are not fundraising. During this time, try to call on each major contributions officer at least once. Tell him what you are doing, your latest accomplishments; ask him for advice on solving a particular problem — do anything except ask him for money. This can be a pleasant and much-appreciated change.

Employee Involvement. You should also try to involve employees of major donors as much as possible. They should be invited to special events. Perhaps you can invite them on a special backstage tour or give them free tickets to a rehearsal. Such efforts will make employees aware of their company's gift and make ongoing company support of your activities important to them.

12

PUTTING IT ALL TOGETHER

The preceding chapters have covered all aspects of a corporate fundraising campaign in considerable detail. The basic steps involved in implementing such a campaign, if one is not already in place, are as follows:

Step 1. Develop the Essential Documents
You cannot raise anything from anyone without telling them what the money is for and why your organization is important. You cannot tell what needs to be raised until you have outlined your plan of action and constructed a realistic budget. Nor can you recruit any volunteers or fully engage your board unless you can tell them exactly what you are and generate enthusiasm for your activities.

Step 2. Outline Your Fundraising History
Only by understanding your organization's past successes and failures can you know the point from which you are starting and whether or not your goals can be achieved. Too often, fund-drive records are in a chaotic state or totally nonexistent. In the latter case you must construct an accurate record of what has happened over the past year or two based on a careful study of the cash receipts book and the correspondence file. How else will you know whom you should approach as a potential first-time giver, and which companies you should look to for renewals?

Step 3. Estimate Your Fundraising Requirements
With your current corporate contributors as a base and using the

factors detailed in Chapter 6, you can make a rough guess of what you will need from old and new prospects to meet your goal. This is by no means the thorough evaluation process you will eventually need to complete, but it will provide a quick, preliminary estimate of the feasibility of your plan and minimize the risk of going through a time-consuming, exhaustive evaluation process only to find that your budget does not work.

For example, you can get an idea of what kind of fund drive is needed by using the following estimates and assumptions: If you are now getting $6,500 from four companies and you need to raise $17,000, and if you assume you would get a 20% increase from all givers, that would give you about $8,000. You still have $9,000 to raise. By dividing $6,500 by four, you can see that current gifts average $1,625 per company. If you get 10% of that average, or about $200 per company, you would need some forty new contributors to get this extra $9,000. Does that seem feasible? To get forty new contributors, you will probably have to solicit 270 companies (based on the 15% success rate mentioned in Chapter 6). Review your estimate yourself, then check it out with your board and others in your community. Is it realistic? Do you think this amount can be raised? If not, you will have to modify your budget.

Step 4. Construct a General Schedule
Once you have an idea of the scope of the campaign that you need to conduct to raise the money you must have, outline the campaign schedule you will have to follow to achieve it. Working backwards from the campaign starting date — using the time allowances of Chapter 10 — you can determine when you must have the campaign materials ready, the volunteers recruited, and the prospect list completed. If you have decided that you must have a certain dollar total from corporations in order to meet your budget and if you have outlined your campaign requirements without major errors, the question to be answered in this analysis is not whether such a campaign can be conducted, but rather what resources are necessary to implement the campaign successfully. If these necessary resources are beyond the capability of your current staff, you should review them with members of

your board to see how they can be obtained. Can special volunteers be recruited or part-time help hired? Are corporate executives available to assist you?

Step 5. Secure Board Approval

At every step in the foregoing analysis, your estimates and assumptions should be gone over carefully with your board president and fund-drive chairman to make sure they are well-informed of what is needed and in agreement with the plans being developed. Once you have created the essential documents, roughed out the fundraising requirements, and outlined a general schedule, you should present the entire package — with all of its assumptions and requirements — to the full board for review, discussion and approval. Board approval, board involvement, board *commitment* are essential to the success of your campaign.

Step 6. Implement the Program

As soon as you have obtained board approval of your overall plan, then you can proceed with the step-by-step development of a corporate fundraising campaign as detailed in this book. You should start by developing a comprehensive fundraising schedule, such as that described in Chapter 10. Doing so will tell you what you should be doing, what you need to accomplish each day to make your campaign a success.

EXHIBITS

EXHIBIT A

ANALYSIS OF CORPORATE CONTRIBUTIONS INFORMATION

This Exhibit contains detailed tables of information compiled from ACA's *Guide to Corporate Giving in the Arts 2*. Even though the data are not necessarily representative of the entire business community, they were derived from information provided by over 500 companies, who volunteered their answers to ACA's special questionnaire.

For those companies the statistics were impressive: 433 companies gave their total contributions budget for all areas, and the figures ranged from a low of $5,000 to a high of $31 million for the year. The average total contributions budget was over $1.3 million. As far as the arts were concerned, the 443 companies who provided answers to this budget question gave a total of nearly $62 million in cash contributions to the arts, *not* counting advertising and other business expenses or non-financial services. This means an average arts contributions budget of $139,858 for the companies who responded.

Percentage of Budget Allocated to the Arts

In terms of the proportion of the total contributions budget allocated to the arts, the overall average for all responding companies was 11.5%, ranging from a low of 0.3% to a high of 86.5%. The following frequency distribution table shows how this ratio differs among companies:

	Companies	
% of Budget	No.	%
0−5	110	25.7
5−10	142	33.2
10−15	76	17.8
15−20	40	9.3
20−25	24	5.6
25−50	30	7.0
50+	6	1.4
Total	428	100.0

Competition for Funds

According to figures comparing the total number of arts requests received with the total number of contributions to the arts by those companies where both figures were available, arts groups have a one-in-four chance of being funded. However, the ratio of gifts to requests (25.2% overall) varies drastically from company to company, as can be seen by the following frequency distribution:

Ratio of Gifts to Requests (%)	Companies No.	Companies %
0 – 10	13	6.0
10 – 20	31	14.2
20 – 30 ·	33	15.1
30 – 40	29	13.3
40 – 50	41	18.8
50 – 60	27	12.4
60 – 70	21	9.6
70 – 80	10	4.6
80 – 90	6	2.8
90 – 100	7	3.2
Total	218	100.0

Caution should be observed in dealing with these figures since less than half the companies in the survey had both sets of data and since the information is for 1979–80.

Branch or Subsidiary Contributions

The average allocation of grants to the corporate headquarters' geographic area was 73.3% for the 363 companies on which data were available. Nearly 10% was allocated to national organizations and 17.1% to subsidiaries and branches.

The frequency distribution shown below indicates the range of these ratios by showing the variation for the home office area.

% Allocated to HQ Area	Companies No.	Companies %
0	25	6.9
1 – 25	19	5.2
25 – 50	32	8.8
50 – 75	50	13.8
75 – 100	123	33.9
100	114	31.4
Total	363	100.0

According to the survey, in only 18.7% of the companies are decisions about contributions made by the field office or branch alone, while 42.1% of the companies reported that decisions were made jointly by the home office and field. Over 39% said they were made by the home office alone.

Application Requirements

Materials required in submitting funding requests for the arts vary from company to company. However, as the following table indicates, certain items are fairly standard.

| | *Companies* | |
Item Required	*No.*	*% of Respondents*
Written Narrative	429	93.1
Complete Budget	356	77.2
IRS Letter of Determination	376	81.6
Application Form	73	15.8
Board List	279	60.5
Contributors List	287	62.3
Audited Statement	267	57.9

Documentation

Only 28.7% of the responding companies issued or planned to issue an annual report on their contributions. A total of 137 companies (29.7%) said they had complete written criteria and applications procedures which were available on request.

Processing Time

It takes an average of almost two months (7.6 weeks) between the time an application is submitted and a final answer is given. This time can, of course, vary depending on the deadlines and overall contributions review cycle. It includes the time that must be allowed for staff review, follow-up questions, and reviews by the appropriate contributions and board committees.

The variations among companies are indicated by the following table:

Processing Time (Months)	Companies No.	%
1	105	29.3
2	161	44.9
3	68	19.0
4	16	4.5
5 or More	8	2.3
Total	358	100.0

Evaluation Criteria

Companies were given a list of fourteen criteria (plus a space to write in "other") and asked to indicate the importance of each in the evaluation of arts requests. A one-to-five scale was used, with one the most important and five the least. The table below summarizes the overall ranking of these criteria according to the number of times each received a one or two.

	Rated one or two	
	No. Companies	% Companies
Impact on Local Community	423	87.6
Geographic Location	419	86.7
Management Capability	326	67.5
Artistic Merit	287	59.5
Employees Involvement	265	54.9
Quality of Application	209	43.3
Board of Directors	186	38.5
Size of Audience	165	34.1
Support by Other Firms	133	27.5
Coordination with Similar Groups	113	23.4
Support by Foundations /Government	75	15.6
Publicity Value	72	14.9
Matching Grants	60	12.4
Gifts from Individuals	39	8.1

EXHIBIT B

SAMPLE OUTLINES

This Exhibit contains two sample outlines developed according to the principles and process described in Chapter 4. The first (Schedule B-1) is for a modern dance company; the second (Schedule B-2) covers a national arts service organization.

SCHEDULE B-1

THE DAVID WILDE DANCE FOUNDATION – OUTLINE

The DAVID WILDE DANCE FOUNDATION is a dance company and school whose purpose is the development of a new level of artistic excellence in modern dance. Through emphasis on the individual dancer, David Wilde's works celebrate human dignity. The special skills and techniques found in his choreography comprise a highly developed technical vocabulary that joins modern dance with ordinary life and themes from the nation's heritage.

Operations

The David Wilde Dance Foundation has three main areas of activity: a modern dance company, dance education, and the development of new works.

David Wilde and Dancers: Given the emphasis on the individual dancer, the performing company is the keystone of the David Wilde Foundation. The *Times* called David Wilde "one of the best dancers of the modern dance scene." Mr. Wilde danced with Martha Graham, Doris Humphrey and Merce Cunningham.

David Wilde's seven-member performing company has been a featured part of the Dance Touring Program of the National Endowment for the Arts for the past six years. In addition to performing in their annual New York season, the Company has toured throughout the United States, Europe, South America, and as part of a special State Department tour of India, Pakistan and Sri Lanka.

Because the Company is small, highly skilled and extensively experienced, and because its performances are based on excellence, not elaborate props with scenic effects, the Company has been able to perform in a wide variety of places before a wide variety of audiences. In fact, performances have been given in over 250 locations to an estimated total audience of 400,000 persons.

Dance Education: The core of the educational operations of the David Wilde Dance Foundation is the Wilde Studio in New York City. At the studio, classes in the Wilde Technique are offered to an average of 600 students a year, a number limited by space and time requirements. The school at the Studio attracts students from France, Switzerland, Finland, Venezuela, Israel, and all parts of the United States. Most students are already professional dancers who are interested in learning the special qualities and skills of David Wilde's technique.

Scholarships are available on a limited basis to those who cannot afford the tuition fee.

In addition to the studio classes, special workshops are given by David Wilde and the company's dancers in other locations around the country. These workshops range from lecture-demonstrations to individual tutoring to classes for entire companies on sections of his repertory.

New Works: The artistic vitality and future of the David Wilde Dance Foundation rest on the development of the new dance pieces.

"David Wilde's choreographic talent is individual, unpredictable, inspired. . . as a dancer he is, as always, a joy to watch. But as a creator he is even more original and exciting." (*International Times*)

In all areas of its activities, the David Wilde Dance Foundation joins artistic excellence and individual creativity into an art of joy and a celebration of the human spirit.

BOARD OF DIRECTORS

Dean Leader, Chairman

Heather Brown	Susan Keyworth
Albert Carlson	Millard Luck
Frank Grace	William Roster
Lester Gross	Jessica Thomas
Mary Hastings	John Washington

SCHEDULE B-2

THE AMERICAN COUNCIL FOR THE ARTS
OUTLINE

*The American Council for the Arts (ACA) is a national arts service organ-
ization, founded in 1960, whose mission is to promote and strengthen cultural
activities in the United States.* ACA's major areas of effort—management improvement and general advocacy—serve to accomplish this mission by helping to
improve internal and external support systems for the arts.

In the area of *management improvement*, ACA seeks to strengthen the internal management of the arts by improving the administrative skills of arts
managers and artists, by providing them with essential managment information,
and by developing management services for their ongoing support.

ACA's *advocacy* efforts are designed to increase the external support of the
arts by demonstrating their importance and by helping both the public and
private sectors develop reasonable policies toward the arts. In addition, ACA
works to build and strengthen alliances within the arts as well as between the arts
and other segments of society.

*ACA carries out its mission by providing a number of products and services
for arts leaders—arts professionals, arts trustees, and arts supporters.* ACA is
unique not only because of its specific activities, but also because *it is the only organization working on behalf of ALL the arts, all across the country.*

ACA carries out its management improvement and advocacy efforts through
four major programs:

1. **Publications.** ACA is the foremost publisher of books for leaders in the arts.
Its publications include "how-to" manuals, statistical surveys, and in-depth
analyses of important topics. Titles include *Financial Management for the
Arts, A Guide to Corporate Giving in the Arts,* and *A Survey of Arts Administration Training.*

American Arts magazine covers a broad range of topics, such as "Issues in
Cultural Policy," "State of the Arts" on important developments in various
disciplines, and "Profiles" of significant artists. ACA *Update* provides information on current events of significance for the arts field.

2. **Conferences and Seminars.** ACA offers seminar packages for use by any
organization wishing to conduct practical workshops for its constituents. Topics include long-range planning and financial management.

Each year ACA holds one major conference, which not only focuses on new
opportunities for the arts, but also helps build new networks of arts support.

Recent examples are "The Arts and Tourism" and "Arts and City Planning."

3. **Political Action.** In addition to analyzing important arts issues, ACA seeks to educate public officials and the general public on the importance of the arts. Although it is not a lobbying organization, ACA does monitor government activities for their impact on the arts at the national, state, and community levels. In developing its policies and advocating its positions, ACA relies on a blend of input from both the artistic community and other segments of society interested in and strongly affected by the arts.

4. **Special Programs.** ACA has three programs designed to provide specific kinds of support services:

    a. **Community Development.** In order to help strengthen local arts support systems, ACA has special service programs for united arts funds, festivals, and advocacy organizations.

    b. **Technical Assistance.** ACA provides frequent consulting services for arts groups and responds to thousands of information requests throughout the year. ACA is also working to improve the business community's non-financial services to the arts.

    c. **Alliance-Building.** Within the arts ACA works with a number of other organizations to address critical issues, to explore the possibility of joint ventures, and to avoid needless duplication of services.

    Outside the arts ACA seeks strong ties with organizations serving other segments of society. The purpose of such alliances is to broaden the exposure of the arts and to make sure that, whenever appropriate, they are addressing the needs of other constituencies.

Through all of these efforts, ACA seeks to demonstrate the importance of the arts, improve their support, and help give them their appropriate place on the list of national, social, and individual priorities.

EXHIBIT C

SAMPLE PLANS OF ACTION

This Exhibit contains the drafts of three plans of action—for a modern dance company (Schedule C-1), national arts organization (Schedule C-2), and an arts council raising money as a united arts fund (Schedule C-3). All three were developed according to the principles described in Chapter 4.

SCHEDULE C-1

THE DAVID WILDE DANCE FOUNDATION PLAN OF ACTION

The David Wilde Dance Foundation is a dance company and school whose purpose is the development of a new level of artistic excellence in modern dance. Through a unique blend of sophisticated choreography and a strong emphasis on the individual dancer, David Wilde's works celebrate human dignity. The special skills and techniques found in his choreography comprise a highly developed technical vocabulary that joins modern dance with ordinary life and themes from the nation's heritage.

Long-Range Goals

The Foundation's goals over the next five years are to achieve the following:

1) Significantly increase earned income from performance fees, tuition and workshops.
2) Substantially expand the repertory of the performing company.
3) Provide subsistence salaries to the artistic and professional staff of the Company.
4) Maintain a continued increase in the artistic and financial strength of the Foundation through improved management, especially in the areas of marketing and development.
5) Upgrade touring performances by developing a self-contained tour production equipment unit.
6) Substantially increase public and private support, financially and nonfinancially, of the work of the Foundation.

FY 1981 Plan of Action

The Foundation will work toward fulfilling its long-range goals during FY 1981 in the following manner:

1) *NATIONAL MARKETING CAMPAIGN:* Continued development and implementation includes preparation and distribution of promotional materials about the Company, representation at booking conferences, advertising and development of sponsor contacts.

2) *EARNED INCOME:* With the assistance of this marketing campaign, increase Company touring by five weeks each year during the next three-year period.

3) *COMPANY REPERTORY:* Expand the repertory with the addition of two new works, increased use of video and rehearsal time, and upgrading two older works to active performance status.

4) *TOUR PRODUCTION:* Attempt to acquire a portable marley dance floor and a sound system to provide better control over performance conditions when on tour.

5) *MANAGEMENT:* Continue efforts of management which since January 1980 has made dramatic improvements in the administration and development of the Foundation's activities at minimal cost.

6) *CORPORATE AND FOUNDATION DRIVE:* Initiate a new drive to substantially increase total contributions. This income, combined with increased earned income, will provide necessary artistic and administrative salary support.

SCHEDULE C-2

THE AMERICAN COUNCIL FOR THE ARTS
PLAN OF ACTION

The American Council for the Arts (ACA) is a national arts service organiza-tion, founded in 1960, whose mission is to promote and strengthen cultural ac-tivities in the United States. ACA's major areas of effort — management improve-ment and general advocacy — serve to accomplish this mission by helping to im-prove internal and external support systems for the arts.

In the area of *management improvement*, ACA seeks to strengthen the inter-nal management of the arts by improving the administrative skills of arts man-agers and artists, by providing them with essential management information, and by developing management services for their ongoing support.

ACA's *advocacy* efforts are designed to increase the external support of the arts by demonstrating their importance and by helping both the public and private sectors develop reasonable policies toward the arts. In addition, ACA works to build and strengthen alliances within the arts as well as between the arts and other segments of society.

ACA carries out its mission by providing a number of products and services for arts leaders — arts professionals, trustees, and arts supporters. ACA is unique not only because of its specific activities, but also because it *is the only organiza-tion working on behalf of ALL the arts, all across the country.*

Long-range Goals

ACA's goals over the next five years are to help achieve the following:

1. A significant improvement in the management of the arts.
2. Increased cooperation among national arts service organizations, social ser-vice agencies, and local arts groups.
3. A substantial increase in financial and nonfinancial support for the arts.
4. The development of a comprehensive body of information on the arts.

FY 1982: Plan of Action

I. *Programs.* ACA has four major programs to carry out its management im-provement and advocacy efforts:

    A. *Publications.* ACA publishes a wide range of books from manuals to statistical surveys and in-depth analyses of major issues. ACA also produces the widely-acclaimed *American Arts* magazine and ACA *Update*. During FY 1982, ACA's efforts in the publications area will include:

1. *American Arts.* ACA will continue its bimonthly magazine, which explores key arts issues and events. The feasibility of expanding the magazine's size and increasing its frequency will be examined. During FY 1982, ACA will increase its advertising and subscription base substantially and will continue to use its multi-discipline Advisory Board.

2. *Books.* New titles under consideration for FY 1982 include the following; an arts management textbook; a landmark book on arts and cities; an updated survey on united arts funds; and an analysis of labor relations in the arts. A total of seven new books will be produced during FY 1982.

3. *ACA Update.* ACA's informative monthly news bulletin will be continued and expanded.

B. *Conferences and Seminars.* During FY 1982 ACA will offer a series of six seminars designed to help other service organizations provide management training to arts administrators in their areas. Topics include long-range planning, fundraising, and financial management.

In the conference area ACA plans to hold a landmark conference on arts and technology in the latter half of FY 1982. Such a conference is designed not only to focus on new opportunities for the arts, but also to help build new alliances and networks of arts support.

ACA is also developing an advanced management conference to provide experienced arts professionals with an opportunity to participate in intensive workshops employing sophisticated techniques and to meet with peers from other disciplines.

C. *Political Action.* In addition to analyzing important arts issues, ACA seeks to educate public officials and the general public on the importance of the arts. Although it is not a lobbying organization, ACA does monitor government activities, since these often have a significant impact on every state and community. In developing its policies and advocating its positions, ACA relies on a blend of input from both the artistic community and from other segments of society interested in and strongly affected by the arts.

During FY 1982 ACA's political efforts will continue to focus on ensuring that government policy towards the arts is fair and that the arts receive their proper place in the list of national priorities. ACA encourages equitable and reasonable financial support for the arts, monitors government activities, and advises arts groups of impending changes.

D. *Special Programs.* ACA's special programs focus on these specific areas which need concentrated effort:

1. *Community Development.* FY 1982 will see a continuation of ACA's comprehensive program of manuals, surveys, conferences, and general assistance for united arts funds, festivals and advocacy organizations.

2. *Technical Assistance.* ACA plans to continue its frequent consultations with arts groups and to use the resources of its staff and 10,000 volume library to respond to the needs of the field. ACA will also work to improve the business community's non-financial services to the arts.

3. *Alliance Building.* In almost every area of its activities, ACA seeks to develop and expand alliance within the arts as well as between the arts and other segments of society.

Integrating the arts into the mainstream of society is one of the most important of ACA's programs. Through the ongoing partnerships it develops with social service agencies outside the arts field, ACA works to infuse the arts into the programs of these organizations and to make sure that the needs of their constituencies are being addressed by the arts. These alliance-building efforts will continue during FY 1982.

II. *Support Systems.* In order to provide these high-quality programs and services at a cost the arts can afford, ACA will continue to improve its own operations:

A. *Administration.* The keystone of all ACA's efforts is improved management. ACA will continue to keep costs at a minimum and to improve the quality of its programs and services.

B. *Earned Income.* Earned income will be increased through a continuing series of high-quality publications and other ACA products. In addition, ACA will develop and implement an effective marketing strategy for these products.

C. *Corporate Drive.* Building on the strong corporate support base developed during FY 1981, ACA will expand its annual business fund drive to include more companies than ever before and increase total contributions to $255,000.

D. *Membership Drive.* ACA will institute a comprehensive membership development campaign during FY 1982. With the effective delivery of top-quality programs and services as its selling point and an intensive marketing effort as its tool, ACA will substantially increase revenue from memberships.

E. *Benefits.* ACA's goal is to hold at least one benefit to produce an estimated $25,000 in revenue during FY 1982.

Through all these efforts, ACA seeks to demonstrate the importance of the arts and improve their support, to enable the arts to make optimum use of contributions and other resources, and to help give them an appropriate place in the list of national, social, and individual priorities.

SCHEDULE C-3

GREATER HARTFORD ARTS COUNCIL
PLAN OF ACTION

The Greater Hartford Arts Council is a service organization. It serves the arts, it serves business, and in so doing it serves the community.

The objective of the Arts Council is to support and extend cultural activities in the Greater Hartford region. The Council's primary means of achieving this objective is to raise money from business in an annual fund drive. In addition, the Council provides technical assistance and other non-financial aid to arts organizations.

The council also serves the business community. Its support of the arts ensures a high quality of life which helps attract good people and firms to the area. Furthermore, the Council's federated appeal frees companies from numerous individual solicitations, and its comprehensive budget review process assures business that all contributions will be well used and fairly distributed.

In short, the Arts Council helps unite business and the arts in a circle of mutual benefit.

I. Long Range Goals

The Greater Hartford Arts Council will accomplish the following over the next five years:

A. A significant broadening of support for the arts through

   1. An expanded fund drive that will include all possible business and professional firms.
   2. The promotion of special fundraising projects and events.
   3. Comprehensive efforts to increase individual, private foundation, and government funding of the arts and the Arts Council.
   4. An expansion of non-financial assistance to the arts by businesses, professionals, and individuals.

B. A substantial improvement in the overall efficiency and effectiveness of arts management by

   1. Helping coordinate activities so as to avoid needless duplication of services, administrative functions, and facilities.
   2. Providing direct technical assistance to arts organizations.
   3. Offering or sponsoring courses on arts management.

C. A significant increase in the public awareness of and involvement in the arts through

1. A general promotional effort that includes the widespread dissemination of materials on the arts and their importance.
2. Direct advocacy efforts by the Council and assistance to arts advocate groups.
3. Assistance to arts groups in the area of marketing and publicity.
4. Encouraging cooperative activities among arts groups, especially on a regional basis.
5. Assistance in the formation of local arts councils and associations.
6. Encouraging arts groups to involve all segments of the community in their activities.

D. The development of a comprehensive arts/education strategy on a region-wide basis that will

1. Help ensure an equal arts opportunity for area children.
2. Develop a long-term audience base for the arts.
3. Help infuse the arts into the mainstream of education.
4. Help optimize the usage of scarce resources.
5. Use arts groups as resources for public schools and use public schools as resources for the arts.

II. Plan of Action: Fiscal Year 1979

In Fiscal 1979, the Greater Hartford Arts Council will continue the process of reexamination and revaluation begun in FY 1978. A special *ad hoc* committee will review and make recommendations to the Arts Council board on such questions as the following:

A. Should the Council solicit individual contributions?

B. What geographic area should the Council serve?

C. Should the Council enlarge its staff in order to provide more services, particularly for small arts groups?

D. How should Council funds be distributed?

E. How should an evaluation of artistic quality be made?

F. Should representatives of arts organizations serve on the Council's board? If so, how many and in what capacity?

Unless they are in conflict with the answers the board adopts to those questions, the Arts Council plans to accomplish the following during FY 1979:

A. *Fund Raising:* The Council will work to continue the increase in financial support for the arts. Specifically, the Council will

1. Raise $625,000 in its fund drive by soliciting 1200 businesses and professional firms with some 350 volunteers.

2. Sponsor the Frank Sinatra concerts on September 4, 5 and 6 as a fundraising benefit.

3. Explore and develop other fundraising projects, such as additional benefit concerts.

4. Seek support from government and private foundation sources for special projects as well as for joint ventures with arts groups.

B. *Services.* The Arts Council will expand its non-financial services to arts organizations in FY 1979 by

1. Expanding and improving the technical assistance offered by the Arts Business Consultants volunteers.

2. Working with arts organizations to help them make the most effective use of the Council's centralized mailing list.

3. Communicating with arts groups on a regular basis in order to properly inform them of important funding deadlines, general events, and Arts Council activities.

4. Working with businesses to increase the number of items and services that can be made available to arts groups.

5. Exploring the availability of federal and other funds and informing arts groups of the procedures necessary to secure them.

6. Offering, in cooperation with the Hartford Graduate Center, a course on business fundamentals for arts administrators.

C. *Arts Advocacy and Promotion:* The Arts Council will continue its efforts to expand public awareness of the arts. Specifically, the Arts Council will

1. Continue its support of the Connecticut Advocates for the Arts.

2. Publish a directory of arts activities in the Greater Hartford area.

3. Establish an annual award for outstanding service to the arts.

D. *Arts and Education.* The Council will continue its efforts to develop a comprehensive arts/education strategy for the Greater Hartford region. The initial emphasis will be on Hartford, with a view toward developing concepts that can be expanded to include the entire area. In FY 1979, the Council will

1. Help State Education consultants analyze arts needs in the Hartford public school system and work with the schools, the Greater Hartford Chamber of Commerce and other agencies in helping satisfy them.

2. Co-sponsor an arts/education showcase for visual and performing arts.

3. Begin to explore ways in which coordination can be increased among schools and arts groups on a regional basis.

E. *Projects and Studies.* During FY1979, the Arts Council will work on three important projects:

1. *Arts Survey.* By December 31, 1978, the Council will complete its survey of arts activities in the region. This survey will provide basis statistics on the

local arts industry, as well as information on arts needs and recommendations as to what functions the Arts Council should perform.

2. *Common Administrative Functions.* With the assistance of the Arts Business Consultants, the Council will begin a comprehensive analysis of potential costs and benefits of cooperative efforts in advertising, purchasing, and other administrative areas.

3. *Arts Liaison/Grant Officer.* Based on the results of the arts survey as well as a pilot project funded by CETA, the Council will explore the need and feasibility of adding an Arts Liaison/Development Officer to its staff in order to

   a. Help arts organizations write grants and develop funding sources.
   b. Provide information, coordination and other services to arts groups on an intensive base.
   c. Increase the communication between the Arts Council and arts organizations.

The successful achievement of all the items in this action plan will produce a truly significant increase in the contributions, effectiveness, and strength of both the arts and the Arts Council.

EXHIBIT D

SAMPLE BUDGETS

This Exhibit contains in Schedule D-1 the budget for the David Wilde Dance Foundation and in Schedule D-2, the annual budget for the American Council for the Arts. Each budget was developed from the organization's plan of action described in Exhibit C.

SCHEDULE D-1

THE DAVID WILDE DANCE FOUNDATION BUDGET

EXPENSES

Artistic Salaries		$ 76,000
Administration		12,500
Professional Fees		8,400
Fringe, Insurance		16,000
Travel		15,500
Studio Rental		8,200
Production Expenses		9,000
Office and Studio Expenses		5,200
Promotion		7,500
Equipment*		17,500
	Total	$ 175,800

INCOME

Performance Fees, Tuition, Workshop Fees		$ 96,800
Individual Contributions		9,000
Corporations		56,500
Foundations		3,500
Government		10,000
	Total	$ 175,800

*One time purchase to reduce costs of rental equipment.

SCHEDULE D-2

AMERICAN COUNCIL FOR THE ARTS BUDGET

	FY82
SUPPORT AND REVENUE	
Publications	88,500
American Arts/Update	39,500
Conferences	55,000
Membership	62,500
Miscellaneous	34,300
Corporations	230,000
Individuals	28,000
Government	57,500
Foundations	25,000
Benefit	34,800
TOTAL	655,100
DIRECT PROGRAM EXPENSE[1]	
Publications	67,600
American Arts/Update	86,300
Conferences	53,300
Membership	9,300
Advocacy	46,800
SUBTOTAL	263,300
GENERAL EXPENSES	
Salaries, Fringe Benefits	239,000
Temporary Help	14,700
Rent	79,200
Telephone	18,500
Postage	3,600
Supplies, Equipment	11,400
Insurance	3,200
Professional Fees	3,000
Travel	8,400
Interest Expense	10,800
SUBTOTAL	391,800
TOTAL	655,100
NET SURPLUS	0

[1]Out of pocket only, not including staff and overhead expenses.

EXHIBIT E

COMPUTER PROSPECT LIST

The computer prospect list for a communitywide fund drive includes basic data that can be sorted and printed out in a variety of ways, as listed below. A format for the list sorted and printed according to team captain and solicitor is presented on the following pages. All programming and running of this list was generously donated by the Burroughs Corporation.

Version	Title	Description
1.	Master list	All data sorted alphabetically by company.
2.	Team list	All data sorted by team, solicitor, and company. Printed one page per solicitor: pages then separated and given to each solicitor.
3.	Team summary	By team, solicitor, solicitor phone number, amount requested, contributions history. One line per prospect. One page per team. Used by captain.
4.	Geographic list	Company name and amount, sorted by town.
5.	Industry list	Company name and amount, sorted by SIC code.
6.	Evaluation list	Company name and amount, sorted by size of evaluation, in descending order.
7.	Labels	Program for properly printing contact name, company, and address on labels and pledge cards.
8.	Contributor list	Alphabetic list of company name only.

Captain	Solicitor	Prospect	SIC	Acct.	Sales	Emp.	Date	Goal	Pledge	Paid	Lst yr	Prv yr
Name Telephone Number	Name Telephone Number	Company Name Address	SIC Code	Acct. No.	Sales ($million)	No. of employees	(1)	Last year's target	(2)	(3)	(4)	(5)
Name Telephone Number	Name Telephone Number	Company Name Address	SIC Code	Acct. No.	Sales ($million)	No. of employees	(1)	Last year's target	(2)	(3)	(4)	(5)
Name Telephone Number	Name Telephone Number	Company Name Address	SIC Code	Acct. No.	Sales ($million)	No. of employees	(1)	Last year's target	(2)	(3)	(4)	(5)

(1) Date on which contribution decision will be made.
(2) To be filled in with dollar amount when a pledge is received.
(3) To be filled in with dollar amount when the contribution is actually received.
(4) Last year's contribution history, coded to show, for example, the name of last year's solicitor, the approximate amount given or the refusal to give, and other such details.
(5) Previous year's contribution history, showing, for example, amount given or refusal, etc.

SCHEDULE E-1
SAMPLE COMPUTER PRINTOUT

EXHIBIT F

SAMPLE APPROACH LETTERS

This Exhibit contains letters drafted for use in several different campaigns:

Schedule F-1: American Council for the Arts Renewal Letter is seeking the renewed support of current contributors and has a slightly different focus than the letter to new prospects shown in Table 5. It also assumes that the recipient has been receiving (and reading) materials from ACA on a regular basis throughout the past year.

Schedule F-2: David Wilde Dance Foundation New Prospect Letter

Schedule F-3: Greater Hartford Arts Council New Prospect Letter: Sample Variations 1 and 2.

All of the above letters were developed on the basis of the materials presented in Exhibits B–D.

AMERICAN COUNCIL FOR THE ARTS

570 Seventh Avenue
New York, New York 10018
212 354-6655
WORKING FOR ALL THE ARTS
NATIONALLY SINCE 1960

Mr. Frank P. Thomas
National Works, Inc.
5024 Fudge Street
Pandora, Wisconsin 57834

Dear Frank:

The contribution National Works gave to ACA helped make 1980–1981 another record year in our efforts to promote and strengthen cultural activities in the United States:

We produced six new books, including our new <u>Guide to Corporate Giving in the Arts</u>, and <u>Americans and the Arts</u> survey. Our <u>American Arts</u> magazine and <u>ACA Update</u> provided essential information to arts professionals, trustees, and supporters. We produced a landmark "Arts and Tourism" conference and special seminars on subjects ranging from financial management to long-range planning. We also increased our linkages with other arts organizations as well as with organizations outside the arts.

With respect to our traditional role as resource to public officials and policy-makers, our reasoned advocacy efforts once again proved welcome, useful and influential. In testimony before Congress, we acknowledged the nation's overall desire to reduce growth in government spending. We argued that the arts are not exempt from the economic realities of the times, but at the same time, we made it plain that it is unrealistic to expect the business community alone to pick up the shortfall.

The best indication of our success has been the response to our efforts. From all over the country, ACA received praise for its activities—not only in the form of letters and calls, but also in more tangible terms: <u>membership increased 50%, American Arts subscriptions went up ten-fold, the number of business contributors increased to over eighty, and publications sales rose by 27%.</u>

ACA is the only national organization working on behalf of <u>all</u> the arts, and this very positive response shows the importance of our efforts in the areas of management improvement and general advocacy—efforts which will be even more essential in the future, as the federal government in resetting priorities, looks increasingly to the private sector organizations like ACA to fill the gap.

SCHEDULE F-1
ACA RENEWAL LETTER

In order for ACA to accomplish this, to carry out our mission, and to provide services at a price the arts can afford, we need your continued support. I hope you will consider an increase to the $5,000 level in order to help us meet the increased demand for our services by arts organizations experiencing difficulties in the new economic environment.

This year your support can give ACA an additional boost. We have applied to the National Endowment for the Arts for a Challenge Grant, which means that any increase in your gift this year will be used to match the grant if it is awarded.

I am enclosing for your information our plan of action for the coming year as well as other background materials on ACA. We would be very pleased to talk with you in person about our current plans and activities.

Thank you very much.

Sincerely,

Eugene F. Dorsey
Corporate Drive Chairman

EFD:et
Enclosures

**THE
DAVID WILDE
DANCE
FOUNDATION**

735 west 23rd street
new york city, new york 10011
212/555-1234
cable address: WILDEBEEST

Mr. E.J. Sloan
Corporate Contributions Officer
Afco Resurfacing Corporation
681 Blount Boulevard
Los Angeles, California 90001

Dear Mr. Sloan:

As you can see by the enclosed materials, the David Wilde Dance Foundation consists of a unique modern dance company and school. Both the company and the school are of exceptionally high artistic quality and are dedicated to advancing the level of excellence in modern dance.

Founded in 1967, the company's efforts have been focused on the development of intricate techniques, the making of sophisticated choreography, and the training of skilled dancers in the unique approach of David Wilde. As a result, the dance company and school have achieved widespread recognition, especially in the dance field, for their artistic excellence. Not only have reviews in such publications as the Times, Dancer's Magazine, and the International Times been exceptionally favorable, but also, there has been a heavy demand for David Wilde's work by both professional dancers and dance companies. For example, dancers with a number of well-known modern dance companies study at the Wilde studio and David Wilde is unable to fill all the requests he receives to commission works for other companies. In addition, word of mouth from previous performances has been sufficient to book fully and quickly each of the eight years of David Wilde's touring program sponsored by the National Endowment for the Arts.

Building on this base of solid accomplishment and support, our goals this year are to reach new audiences to a total of 60,000 people across the country, and to carry out an aggressive marketing campaign to broaden the company's support, increase its visibility, and strengthen its financial position.

BOARD OF DIRECTORS
Dean Leader
Chairman
Heather Brown
Albert Carlson
Frank Grace
Lester Gross
Mary Hastings
Susan Keyworth
Millard Luck
William roster
Jessica Thomas
John Washington

To help us achieve our goals, we hope that Afco Resurfacing Corporation will give favorable consideration to a grant of $10,000 to the David Wilde Dance Foundation. Such a gift would have a substantial effect and would ensure our success in reaching new audiences, increasing our visibility, and encouraging other corporations to support our efforts.

SCHEDULE F-2

DAVID WILDE DANCE FOUNDATION NEW PROSPECT LETTER

In short, Afco Resurfacing's assistance at this critical juncture in the history of the David Wilde Dance Foundation will help it to reach its high potential of artistic excellence and widespread impact. Naturally, such support would receive appropriate and full recognition in all literature, programs, and other materials of the Foundation.

Please let me know if you need any additional information on the company. I look forward to hearing from you.

Sincerely,

Dean Leader
Chairman
Board of Directors

Greater Hartford Arts Council

W. Grant Brownrigg
Executive Director

250 Constitution Plaza
Hartford, Connecticut 06103
(203) 525-8629

[Date]

[Name of Contact
Name of Corporation
Address]

Dear

67% of the executives interviewed in a recent national survey said that business has a responsibility to help support cultural activities in their community. They recognized that the arts are important in terms of providing

1. A high quality of life, which helps recruit good people.
2. A large number of skilled teachers.
3. A key attraction for tourists and conventions.
4. Direct economic benefits—jobs and local purchases— estimated at over $28 million per year in our state.

In Greater Hartford, we are fortunate in having local groups that are excellent in quality. . . . But they need your support.

As you can see by the enclosed brochure, the Arts Council is working to help the arts in our region. Within a few days, someone will be contacting you to ask for your help in our current fund drive. I hope you will join us in our effort.

I think an important point to consider is that any contribution you make will be matched on a 1 to 3 basis by the federal government, if the National Endowment's challenge grant is awarded to the Council. Thus, each dollar you give may produce $1.33 for the arts in Greater Hartford.

Sincerely,

Marvin S. Loewith
Fund Drive Chairman

Enclosure

Organized by the Greater Hartford Chamber of Commerce

SCHEDULE F-3
SAMPLE APPROACH LETTER: VARIATION 1

Greater Hartford Arts Council

W. Grant Brownrigg
Executive Director

250 Constitution Plaza
Hartford, Connecticut 06103
(203) 525-8629

[Date]

[Name of Contact
Name of Corporation
Address]

Dear

The [year] fund drive for the Greater Hartford Arts Council is underway. I am writing you to ask for your continued financial support so that together we can help maintain the unique quality of life in our area.

The Arts Council not only serves as a conduit for financial assistance to the arts, but it also provides a valuable review and challenge function. Through the volunteer efforts of a large group of business executives, administrative costs are being streamlined and marketing skills are being employed to attract larger audiences.

The recent Frank Sinatra Concert at the Civic Center was an artistic and financial success. We plan to have at least one more such event so that the combined proceeds will offset the entire administrative costs of the Arts Council. This would mean that 100% of every dollar contributed by the business community will go directly to the various arts organizations.

Specifically, we are asking that [Name of Corporation] consider carefully a contribution of $[amount] to the Greater Hartford Arts Council for its [year] fund drive.

We'll be in touch with you in a few days to answer any questions not answered by this letter and the attached descriptive materials.

Sincerely,

Marvin S. Loewith
Fund Drive Chairman

Organized by the Greater Hartford Chamber of Commerce

SCHEDULE F-3
SAMPLE APPROACH LETTER: VARIATION 2

EXHIBIT G

SAMPLE SOLICITOR KIT

This exhibit contains a sample of the materials given to each solicitor at the kick-off meeting of the Greater Hartford Arts Council's fund drive.

Schedule G-1 is the Table of Contents for both the solicitor kit and the other schedules.

Where available, articles on prospects were included in the appropriate solicitor's kit along with any other special information or facts that might be needed (such as the importance of the arts to a particular, remote town where a prospect is located).

SCHEDULE G-1

TABLE OF CONTENTS

SCHEDULE G-2

FUND DRIVE
APPROACH & METHODOLOGY

I. **Overall Approach**
  A. Soliciting contributions is very much like sales. Personal contact and product knowledge are the key ingredients.
    1. **Personal contact.** Please try to arrange for a personal visit to each prospect. Nothing is as effective as a face-to-face discussion, and your willingness to take time to do so shows your strong support of the Council's work. Also, it is essential that a prospective contributor know how valuable the arts are to the community. His awareness of their importance will have more beneficial results for the arts over the long term than a check written only to placate a solicitor.
    2. **Product knowledge.** Please read the materials provided you on the arts and the Arts Council so that you are well informed. If you need any further information, please call the staff [tel. no.].
  B. Several important points to keep in mind.
    1. This is a "one-gift-for-the-arts" appeal; no other approach will be made this year.
    2. You are asking for an *investment* in the community, one that has high returns for business — not begging for a hand-out.
    3. Our local arts organizations are nationally renowned and have a far better earnings record than the U.S. average. Yet by their very nature, they are not able to support themselves.

II. **Suggested Methodology**
  A. Contact your prospects the first day that you have your pledge cards.
    1. Refer to Bud Loewith's letters (copies enclosed).
    2. Ask for an opportunity to discuss the Arts Council in a 10–15 minute personal interview (sample script enclosed).
    3. You may wish to use one of the 3 sample letters enclosed as an initial "introduction" to be followed up by a telephone call or personal visit.
  B. The Personal Interview.
    1. Suggested outline is attached. It is based on the white paper, slide presentation, and other materials given each solicitor.
    2. Try to "close the sale" at the time of the interview.
      a. Fill out the pledge card and ask prospect to sign it, then you sign it.
    3. Leave with the prospect.
      a. Annual Report.
      b. Copy of newspaper article on Advocate Action Committee.
      c. Decal.

4. Notify the Council if the prospect desires additional information.

C. Send thank you letter (sample attached). The Council will send an "official" thank you but a personal one from you would be important.

III. **Procedures**

A. Please contact your prospects and follow up as soon as possible. Quick action means the job is finished and out of the way with a minimum of effort.

1. Please fill out the Solicitor Report Form and send it in.

2. Self-addressed envelopes are provided for your use and that of your prospects.

B. The computer printout gives the best information that was available to the staff. Please verify this data wherever possible and note corrections and additions in the "Comments" column of the Report Form. All information will be invaluable for next year.

C. Tell your captain immediately if you're having problems with a prospect, so it can be reassigned if necessary.

SCHEDULE G-3

SAMPLE TELEPHONE APPROACH

Solicitor: Hello my name is _____. Several days ago, Bud Loewith wrote to you about the Arts Council. I'm following up on his letter and would like 10 or 15 minutes of your time to talk with you about the Council.

Prospect: But I'm not interested in the arts!

Solicitor: I can understand that. Many of the businessmen who support the Council are not really interested in the arts themselves. They're interested in the *community*. Since the arts are important to the community, they feel it's important to support the arts. It's like investing money or buying inventory — you do it for the returns you expect to get, not for the sake of getting rid of your money.

Prospect: I don't have time to see you.

Solicitor: I'm only asking for 10 or 15 minutes. I'd like you to understand what we're doing. Even if you don't wish to contribute I'd like you to know about the arts and the Arts Council. I think it's important. That's why I'm calling you, that's why *I'm* taking the time to help the Council.

Prospect: Can't you do it over the phone?

Solicitor: No. It's important that I see you. I have information I'd like to show you. I'm only asking for 10 or 15 minutes.

Prospect: Can't you mail things to me?

Solicitor: It will actually take less time if I stop in and go over things with you for 10 or 15 minutes. I can give you the highlights and a good, overall understanding in that time, then leave information for you to peruse at your leisure.

Greater Hartford Arts Council

W. Grant Brownrigg
Executive Director

250 Constitution Plaza
Hartford, Connecticut 06103
(203) 525-8629

Dear   :

As Bud Loewith pointed out in his recent letter to you, the arts are very important to both business and the community.

The Arts Council is currently conducting its annual "one-gift-for-the-arts" fund drive. As one of the solicitors for the drive, I will be in touch with you in a few days to talk with you about our efforts.

Sincerely,

Organized by the Greater Hartford Chamber of Commerce

SCHEDULE G-4
SAMPLE SOLICITOR LETTER

SCHEDULE G-5

PERSONAL INTERVIEW OUTLINE

I. **Arts Council**
   A. Organized 5 years ago.
   B. Provides funds and in-kind services to arts groups in Greater Hartford.
   C. Endorsed by the Chamber of Commerce.

II. **Arts Supported by Council**
   A. Six receive ongoing support:
      1. Wadsworth Atheneum
      2. Hartford Symphony
      3. Hartford Ballet Company
      4. Connecticut Opera
      5. Hartford State Company
      6. Hartford Chamber Orchestra
   B. Civic & Arts Festival
   C. Community Arts & Education groups like Artists Collective, Peace Train, and the North End Dance Troupe.

III. **State of Arts**
   A. Excellent quality.
   B. Better earnings ratio than the U.S. average.

IV. **Arts are important**
   A. To business
      1. Quality of life helps in recruiting.
      2. Tourists and conventions.
      3. Stimulates creativity in all areas.
      4. Direct economic impact ($4 million).
   B. To society
      1. Enrich individual lives.
      2. Good teachers for our children.
      3. Help to the underprivileged.
      4. Cultural heritage.

V. **Arts Council Activities**
   A. Fund Raising
      1. Corporations: "one-gift-for-the-arts".
      2. Private foundations.
      3. Special events.

B. Strategic Planning
   1. Apply business techniques to increase revenue and decrease costs.
   2. Marketing plan to expand audiences.
C. Improving assistance and coordination
   1. Advocate Action Committee Study: to see if any functions can be combined.
   2. Expanded in-kind services for any applicant arts group

VI. **Conclusion**
   A. Arts and Arts Council working hard to help themselves, but they can't do it alone. Need your support.
   B. Goal is $525,000. This is not the entire amount needed but a minimum necessary to enable groups to maintain essential services.
   C. Specifically, we are asking you to consider a contribution of $_____.

VII. **Closing**
   A. (Ask prospect to sign pledge card.)
   B. (Leave Annual Report, newspaper article, and decal.)
   C. Thank you.

ARTS ARE NOT JUST FOR THE ELITE FEW

I. **Survey Statistics**
   A. 84% of the people interviewed in a recent nationwide poll by Lou Harris agreed that "arts and cultural activities are as important for a community to have as libraries, schools, parks and recreational activities."
   B. According to a telephone survey of 618 people in Greater Hartford, 48% of the people with incomes of less than $10,000 per year and 45% of those with a high school education or less have made use of the Wadsworth Atheneum, for example.

II. **Arts Council Activities**
   A. All of the organizations receiving substantial funding from the Council have special programs to serve children, students, the poor and disadvantaged.
   B. In addition, the Council sponsors the annual Civic & Arts Festival on Constitution Plaza. It is entirely free and draws an estimated 100,000 people each year.
   C. The Council also provides substantial funding to small arts groups whose primary activities are in one or more of the following areas:
   . . . Education
   . . . Aid to the poor and disadvantaged
   . . . Service to young people
   . . . Programs for older adults
   This direct funding is in addition to the many hours of in-kind services provided these small groups by the Council staff as well as the Advocates Action Committee.

SCHEDULE G-7

QUESTIONS & ANSWERS

I. **What is the quality of the arts in our area?**
Excellent. As examples:
A. The Hartford Stage Company's "All Over" was on public television last year. It received excellent reviews by the *Wall Street Journal* and *New York Times.*
B. The Wadsworth Atheneum's collection of paintings contains works by almost every major artist—like Rembrandt, Trumbull, Picasso, and Wyeth—as well as one of five Caravaggios in the country.
C. The Hartford Symphony is second only to the Boston Symphony in New England. It puts on over 30 performances each year, including special concerts for students, ethnic groups and older adults.
D. The Hartford Ballet is the most active touring ballet company in America. Last spring, its leading dancer was a featured performer with the Joffrey in New York, to the rave reviews of the New York papers.
E. The Connecticut Opera Association is the only professional opera company producing grand opera in Connecticut. In fact, it was the 13th professional company to be founded in this country.
F. The Hartford Chamber Orchestra has performed on WQXR in New York and with the Paul Taylor Dance Company at a world premiere in Newport.

II. **Can't the arts support themselves?**
No. The level of costs for the arts is set by the general economy, where productivity improvements can be instituted to offset increases. But such improvements are not possible for the arts—a play or symphony written 200 years ago still has to be handcrafted, still requires the same number of performers, as it did then. Increasing admission charges commensurate with costs would not only limit public access to the arts but would also tend to be self-defeating, in that the resultant prices would be far above what people would be willing to pay. The difference between costs and earned revenues must be made up by contributions.

III. **How do the arts in Hartford compare to the rest of the nation?**
Better. The major organizations in Hartford all earn a higher percentage of their operating budget than the national average for comparable groups. In Hartford, earned income averages about 65% of operating budgets. The Arts Council provides about 6% of the average budget; the remainder is obtained from individual contributions, private foundations, and government grants.

IV. **Why should business support the arts?**
   A. First, it's good business.
      1. Arts improve the quality of life. This makes it easier for companies to attract and keep good people.
      2. The arts help bring tourists and conventions to Hartford.
      3. Creativity is essential to business. Graphics and design are only the most obvious examples. The whole process of management is founded on creativity. A vital arts community provides the training and stimulus for creative people in all fields.
      4. The arts comprise a $4 million local industry, employing hundreds of local people and providing substantial direct stimulus to the regional economy.
   B. Second, the arts are important to society.
      1. They enrich our individual lives, whether we take lessons or go to concerts or attend visual and performing events in our area.
      2. Our children have good teachers — for piano, for drawing, for all the fine arts — because there are good artists in our area, drawn to Greater Hartford by the vitality of our cultural climate.
      3. The arts help the underprivileged. They ameliorate the brutality of an impersonal existence for the elderly, for the poor, for the disadvantaged of all kinds.
      4. One of our richest assets is our cultural heritage; we should not deny our children and future generations this same advantage.

V. **Why should contributions be made to the Arts Council instead of directly to the various arts?**
   A. The Arts Council is a united appeal. "One Gift for the Arts" means one solicitation, one contribution.
   B. The Council has four budget review committees, who carefully review arts organizations and their budgets. These volunteer committees, consisting of top level business executives and other concerned citizens ensure that these organizations are running lean and that contributions are going where they do the most good.
   C. The Arts Council provides in-kind services that help all arts groups operate more efficiently and effectively.
      1. Its Advocate Action Committee of business managers works directly with arts groups to improve their operations.
      2. The Council has specific programs to help arts groups increase their impact and revenues.

SCHEDULE G-8

SOLICITOR REPORT FORM

Solicitor _____

Team _____
Vice Chairman _____

Prospect	Goal	Pledge	Paid	Data Verification	Comments
				1. Right Contact ___ 2. Employees ___ 3. Sales ___ 4. Other ___	
				1. Right Contact ___ 2. Employees ___ 3. Sales ___ 4. Other ___	
				1. Right Contact ___ 2. Employees ___ 3. Sales ___ 4. Other ___	

ABOUT THE AMERICAN COUNCIL FOR THE ARTS

The American Council for the Arts (ACA) is a national arts service organization founded in 1960 whose mission is to promote and strengthen cultural activities in the United States.

In the area of management improvement, ACA seeks to strengthen the internal management of the arts by improving the administrative skills of arts managers and artists by providing them with essential management information and by developing management services for their ongoing support.

ACA's advocacy efforts are designed to increase the external support of the arts by demonstrating their importance and by helping both the public and private sectors to develop reasonable policies toward the arts. In addition, ACA works to build and strengthen alliances within the arts as well as between the arts and other segments of society.

ACA carries out its mission by providing a number of products and services for arts leaders — arts professionals, trustees, and supporters. ACA is the only organization working on behalf of *all* the arts, all across the country.

7414